NAFSA's
International Student Recruitment

EDITED BY

Marie O'Hara

Karen Raftus

Joann Stedman

NAFSA

ASSOCIATION OF
INTERNATIONAL EDUCATORS
WASHINGTON, DC

NAFSA: Association of International Educators promotes the exchange of students and scholars to and from the United States. The association sets and upholds standards of good practice and provides professional education and training that strengthen institutional programs and services related to international educational exchange. NAFSA provides a forum for discussion of issues and a network for sharing information as it seeks to increase awareness of and support for international education in higher education, in government, and in the community.

International Standard Book Number: 0-912207-84-1

Library of Congress Cataloging-in-Publication Data

NAFSA's guide to international student recruitment / edited by Marie O'Hara, Karen Raftus, Joann Stedman.
    p. cm.
    ISBN 0-912207-84-1
    1. Students, Foreign--Recruiting--United States. 2. College students--Recruiting--United States. I. Title: Guide to international student recruitment. II. O'Hara, Marie. III. Raftus, Karen. IV. Stedman, Joann Bye. V. NAFSA: Association of International Educators (Washington, D.C.).

LB2342.82 .N24 2000
378.1'982691--dc21

00-030541

CONTENTS

ACKNOWLEDGMENTS

This book was conceived, crafted, and written by a number of the most experienced professionals in the admission and student services fields-individuals who have shaped the recruitment policies and procedures of colleges and universities across the United States.

Thanks in particular should go to a number of people who were instrumental in the development of this publication, including the members of the advisory board, who served as the architects of the book; to the authors for agreeing to contribute, despite grueling schedules, and for generously sharing the secrets of their trade; and to the reviewers for their thoughtful suggestions. This book has benefited much from the expertise and dedication of my wonderful co-editors, Karen Raftus and Joann Stedman.

Finally, recognition must be given to NAFSA's publications department and, in particular, Steven Kennedy and Megan O'Reilly, for supervising and supporting the creative process.

Marie O'Hara

Chapter 4.3, by Theresa Carroll Schweser, is adapted from articles that appeared in College Board 1994 *Admission Strategist* 21, Fall.

CONTRIBUTORS

At the time of completion of the manuscript.

Advisory Board

Edward Devlin
Monterey, CA

Linda Heaney
President
Linden Educational Services
Washington, DC

Johnny Johnson
Director, International Student Programs
Monterey Peninsula College
Monterey, CA

Fred Lockyear
President
International Advisory Services
Bellevue, WA

Alan Margolis
Independent Consultant
Flushing, NY

June Noronha
Associate Dean for Multicultural Education
College of Saint Catherine
St. Paul, MN

Mary Peterson
Director of Development
College of Nursing
Montana State University
Bozeman, MT

Cassandra Pyle
Retired Executive Director
Council for International Exchange of
    Scholars
Boulder, CO

Donald F. Ross
Director, Center for International Education
Salem State College
Salem, MA

Marjorie Smith
Director of International Admission
University of Denver
Denver, CO

Robert Watkins
Assistant Director of Admissions
University of Texas at Austin
Austin, TX

Valerie Woolston
Director, International Education Services
University of Maryland
College Park, MD

Authors

Audree Chase
Coordinator of International Services
American Association of Community
    Colleges
Washington, DC

Stephen C. Dunnett
Professor and Vice Provost for International
    Education
State University of New York at Buffalo
Buffalo, NY

Clark Egnor
Assistant Executive Director
Center for International Programs
Marshall University
Huntington, WV

Charles Foster
Vice President Emeritus
ELS Language Centers
Culver City, CA

Jim Frey
President
Educational Credential Evaluators, Inc.
Milwaukee, WI

Louis Gecenok
Director, International Student Programs
Saint Mary's College of California
Moraga, CA

Marjory Gooding
Foreign Student Adviser
University of Colorado-Boulder
Boulder, CO

Linda Heaney
President
Linden Educational Services
Washington, DC

Lisa Jacobson
Consultant
Washington, DC

Johnny Johnson
Director, International Student Programs
Monterey Peninsula College
Monterey, CA

Judith Jurek
Assistant Director of International
   Admissions
University of Southern California
Los Angeles, CA

Robert Lawrence
Director
LD&A/SWT Education
Melbourne, Australia

Marsha Lee
Director
Institute of International Education
Hong Kong

JoAnn McCarthy
Dean of International Affairs
University of South Florida
Tampa, Florida

June Noronha
Associate Dean for Multicultural Education
College of Saint Catherine
St. Paul, MN

Elisabeth O'Connell
Director of International Admissions
University of Pennsylvania
Philadelphia, PA

Peggy Printz
Editor and Publisher
Study in the USA
Seattle, WA

Mark Reid
Director, International Admissions
University of Miami
Coral Gables, FL

Liz Reisberg
Consultant
International Strategies and Training
Arlington, MA

John Rogers
Student Adviser, Office of International
   Education and Services
University of Iowa
Iowa City, IA

Theresa Carroll Schweser
Associate Director of International Education
The College Board
Washington, DC

Conrad J. Sharrow
Independent Consultant
Niskayuna, NY

Joann Stedman
Consultant
Stedman Associates
New York, NY

Scott Stevens
Director of ESL
University of Delaware
Newark, DE

Therese Tendick
Associate Dean of Admissions
Thunderbird, The American Graduate School
   of International Management
Glendale, AZ

Greg Walker
President
GTW Consultants
Pittsburgh, PA

Editors

Marie O'Hara
Educational Consultant
New Milford, CT

Karen Raftus
Ohio Wesleyan University
Delaware, OH

Joann Stedman
Consultant
Stedman Associates
New York, NY

Reviewers

Alan Adelman
Director, Educational Counseling Center
Institute of International Education
Mexico City, Mexico

Robert Bray
Director, English Language Center
Old Dominion University
Norfolk, VA

Carl de Angelis
Assistant Director, Preacademic Programs
Institute of International Education
New York, NY

Karlene N. Dickey
Associate Dean of Graduate Studies Emerita
Stanford University
Stanford, CA

Rebecca Dixon
Associate Provost of University Enrollment
Northwestern University
Evanston, IL

Debbie Hefferon
Independent Consultant
Washington, DC

Nancy Keteku
Regional Educational Advising Coordinator-
 Africa
USIS
Accra, Ghana

Norma King
Director, English Language Center
University of Denver
Denver, CO

Frank Falcetta
Associate Provost
Middlesex Community College
Bedford, MA

Juleann Fallgatter
Director, Field Affairs Division
AMIDEAST
Washington, DC

Jon Lea Fimbres
Regional Educational Advising Coordinator-
 Middle East and North Africa
USIS
Magles El Shaab, Egypt

Thomas LePere
Associate Director of Admission
Marymount College
Los Verdes, CA

Maria Lesser
Regional Educational Advising Coordinator-
 Mexico, Central America, Caribbean
USIS
Mexico City, Mexico

Peggy Printz
Editor and Publisher
Study in the USA
Seattle, WA

Henry Scott
Former Regional Educational Advising
 Coordinator-Newly Independent States
USIS

Joe Sevigny
Director
Graduate Enrollment Services
Graduate School of Arts and Science
New York University
New, NY

Lydia Shevchik
Former Regional Educational Advising
 Coordinator-East Central Europe
USIS

Marti Thomson
Regional Educational Advising Coordinator-
 East Asia
USIS
Kuala Lumpur, Malaysia

Joseph Williams
Coordinator of International Alumni
 Relations
State University of New York at Buffalo
Buffalo, NY

FOREWORD

Recruitment scandals of the late 1970s pushed NAFSA: Association of International Educators into a very public arena where it had not been previously. The association had no background papers or policy positions on this issue. In fact, the association and its thousands of members had little or no experience with the recruitment of international students. There were no ground rules or standards of acceptable practice. Many members viewed recruiting as unacceptable. The association's professional emphasis was on managing admissions and subsequent services for students who by their own networks, families, and friends, found their way to U.S. colleges and universities.

The publication of this guide is a culmination of almost two decades of discussion about and actual practice with responsible recruitment. In the early years, some international educators felt uneasy about the very concept of recruitment. Looking back, those feelings were undoubtedly colored by the tawdry examples of recruitment that had made national headlines.

This guide is more than just a superb "how-to" publication. The introduction on marketing with a global perspective and chapter 1.1, a historical background on recruitment, are important readings for NAFSA members and nonmembers alike. Chapter 1.2 addresses the importance of ethical behavior, a cornerstone of NAFSA's efforts to develop sound, responsible recruiting practices.

Recruitment does not exist in a vacuum. Global conditions that affect potential new markets and generate new wealth, the competition these conditions generate in other major recruiting countries, as well as the disastrous financial downturns that can occur will affect your recruiting efforts.

The contributors to this guide bring a wealth of experience to recruitment as we now know it. They are seasoned professionals who have much good advice to share. The practical information they offer will help institutions and individuals charged with developing a recruitment plan. Should you recruit at all? Who are your potential partners on campus? What options are available to you as you build your recruitment plan? College fairs, educational tours, direct mail, and many other techniques are discussed in detail, and many resources and recruiting networks are identified. Regional profiles and sample questionnaires to help you target potential students and collect information are provided.

There is no one model for successful recruiting, nor are there only a few. It would be a testimony to the effectiveness of this guide if you would use its content to develop a multiplicity of approaches that reflect the great diversity of our institutions. No matter what models are developed, they must evolve as institutional conditions change, and as international forces change. Had this publication been released six months ago, two years ago, or ten years ago, the international scene would have cast a very different prediction for recruitment strategies.

Recruitment efforts must be viewed as cumulative. They build long-term relationships between an institution and a network of countries, universities, and individuals. The long-term commitment of the college or university to recruit students from a particular area can sow seeds for generations of students to come. We may be too new at recruitment efforts to see very far into the future. But institutions in the United States, as well as in other countries will continue to seek talented international students. And the desire of students to study abroad will surely continue in its present form, undoubtedly influenced by new means of mobility and information gathering. If we conduct our recruitment activities in a highly professional manner, the educational experience will be beneficial for all parties.

Having participated in the debate over recruitment at the end of the 1970s and having observed so much of what NAFSA has done in the intervening years to reach the point of publishing this guide, I feel enormous satisfaction that this compendium of history, ethical considerations, and practical information will now be shared with thousands of individuals, colleges, and universities. Our recruiting efforts will be stronger for it.

Cassie Pyle

Marketing Higher Education: A Global Perspective

JoAnn S. McCarthy

Throughout history students have left their homes in the pursuit of knowledge. Motivated by the search for intellectual development, spiritual enlightenment, political leadership, social prestige, and economic success, many have traveled great distances to study in foreign lands. Recently student mobility has become a subject of intense interest in the world of higher education, as the "export of educational services" has become a significant item in the national trade account of a half-dozen countries and competition for market share has become significantly more intense, particularly among the English-speaking nations of the United States, Australia, Canada, and the United Kingdom.

Global Trends in Higher Education

Several worldwide trends will provide the context and impetus for student mobility in the early years of the twenty-first century.

- The number of students pursuing university studies abroad will double from 1.5 million by 2010.

- Regionalism, exemplified by the European Community Action Scheme for the Mobility of University Students (ERASMUS), the North American Free Trade Agreement (NAFTA), the Association of Southeast Asian Nations (ASEAN), and other trade alliances and networks, will spawn more collaborative efforts in education, thereby increasing student mobility.

- More institutions of higher education will develop their own academic programs abroad in conjunction with partner universities.

- The field of international student affairs will continue to grow and professionalize, as reflected in the growing number of staff in universities, government offices, and placement agencies with special expertise to facilitate student mobility.

- Academic mobility will become increasingly commercialized and competitive, especially in the higher education systems in the United States, Australia, Canada, and the United Kingdom.

- The academic world will grow more anglicized as English-speaking countries compete to attract international students and non-English speaking countries deliver courses of study in English to be more competitive in the education marketplace.

- International accreditation and quality assurance organizations will further standardize the content and delivery of higher education.

- Education consumers will become more informed and value conscious.

- Advances in technology will spread delivery of degree programs via the Internet, satellite, and videotape (Bode 1997).

Factors Affecting Student Mobility and National Competitiveness

The ebb and flow of students from one part of the world to another is influenced by a complex and dynamic interaction of variables, both at home and abroad, including demographics, economic factors, political climate, educational infrastructures, technology, popular perceptions, and formal policies of institutions and governments.

Within that shifting matrix of demand, incentives, and constraints, international students are recruited in a variety of ways, from the aggressive and highly effective efforts of the Australians to the passive approach of countries that have no interest in or capacity to accommodate increased numbers of international students. The level and nature of government involvement in the marketing of higher education also varies widely.

In Australia, arguably the most aggressive higher education system in the realm of international recruitment, officials hope to increase foreign student enrollments by 20 percent per year (Blight 1997). Today international students drawn primarily from nearby Southeast Asian countries comprise fully 10 percent of enrollments in higher education in that country. The Australian government has established a system of education information centers throughout Southeast Asia to support university efforts to market educational programs. These centers, originally established by the Australian International Education Foundation as "a means of linking education, training, and research with trade, investment, and diplomacy," provide generic educational nformation to students, often referring them to agents representing specific nstitutions for further detailed information (Rubin 1996). Australian nstitutions routinely participate in well-attended education fairs, arrange ace-to-face interviews with prospective students, negotiate "articulated ransfer" programs with foreign institutions (including 1+2 and 2+1 degree programs), offer entire degree programs offshore, and work with networks of agents who represent their institutions full time in various countries and regions of the world. IDP-Education Australia, a not-for-profit organization owned by Australian universities, operates another network of offices and franchised operations throughout the world. IDP and a growing population of private agents recruit students on a commission basis for member universities.

The United Kingdom and Canada also have established education networks abroad to assist in attracting international students to their colleges and universities. International students comprise 12 percent of higher education enrollments in the United Kingdom and nearly 6 percent of enrollments in Canada. Both the British and Canadian governments have recognized the economic potential of marketing their institutions of higher education abroad and have instituted policies consistent with that goal. The Educational Counseling Service (supported by subscriber fees paid by 260 British institutions), and the Canadian Education Centre network (supported by the Asia Pacific Foundation, the Department of Foreign Affairs and International Trade, and the Canadian International Development Agency) assist their member institutions in promoting British and Canadian education programs to prospective students worldwide through education fairs, market research, and organized missions of educators who counsel prospective students in their home countries.

Despite its decentralized approach to recruitment, the United States still attracts by far the largest number of international students of any country in the world. Nearly 500,000 international students are enrolled in U.S. institutions, where they comprise 3.2 percent of enrollments, barely one-third the proportion of internationals enrolled in the Australian, British, French, and German systems.

In keeping with a decentralized system of higher education, international student recruitment in the United States is undertaken primarily by individual institutions and is highly idiosyncratic depending on the type of institution, the level of financial resources available, and the availability of staff to undertake such activities. Some institutions regularly take part in commercially sponsored education fairs overseas; some employ agents on behalf of the institution; increasing numbers of institutions are developing transfer agreements and exploring distance-education options; and some send representatives overseas to recruit on a routine basis. Many institutions do not address the issue at all, either in policy or action.

U.S. institutions are supported by a network of nearly 450 overseas educational advising centers that provide impartial information on the full range of options in higher education to more than two million prospective students each year. These centers do not recruit or serve as agents for individual institutions, however. U.S. government support for this far-flung network of educational advisers—totaling some $3 million per year—is channeled through the U.S. Information Agency's Advising, Teaching, and Student Support Services Division. In recent years, advising center budgets have been decreasing, some centers have been forced to close, and most remaining centers are searching for new ways to fund their activities. To make up for cuts in contributions from the U.S. government, the Finland-U.S. Educational Exchange Commission in Helsinki, which manages the Fulbright program in Finland, recently began advising Finnish students on higher-education programs in countries other than the United States.

A closer look at developing patterns in international student mobility reveals that fundamental changes have been taking place over the past decade. While international student numbers continue to grow slightly in the United States, the growth rate has flattened in recent years (Davis 1998). At the same time, Australia and the United Kingdom are showing significant increases in student flows.

Three factors seem to contribute significantly to strengthening the competitiveness of institutions of higher education for the global pool of students.

- Recognition at the regional and national levels of the cultural and economic importance of international student flows often portends more substantive governmental support for coordinated national efforts to attract more international students to academic institutions (Kälvermark, 1997a).

- The development of intermediary organizations allows institutions to pool resources to develop overseas infrastructures in support of aggressive and sophisticated campaigns to attract students to member institutions' campuses.

- Institutional investment in personnel and operating budgets for international recruiting allows a university to market programs abroad in a variety of effective ways ranging from web pages and online application procedures to on-site recruitment campaigns. Furthermore, those institutions that have made provisions for a portion of international student tuition fees to be channeled directly to affected academic departments and international support services are experiencing significant growth due to enthusiastic participation of staff who are motivated by this income stream (Kälvermark, 1997b).

Clearly, educational systems that have addressed all three levels of support for international student recruitment have a decided advantage in the increasngly intense competition for market share in the years ahead. When all three levels of support intersect, institutions can maximize limited resources, offer incentives, eliminate unnecessary barriers, provide convenient access to appropriate information, streamline application and visa procedures, recruit aggressively in well-researched markets, and provide quality academic programs and support services at competitive prices. Such institutions will most likely find large numbers of students who may eagerly enroll and contribute significantly to the campus culture as well as to the local and national economies.

The long-term consequences of ignoring such support factors in a competitive environment could soon become strikingly evident as we continue to assess student flows in the decades to come. Concurrently, the commercialization of higher education and intense competition carry the seeds of potential abuse, which could threaten the integrity of institutions as well as the welfare of international students. International educators who promote student mobility can contribute to the quality of higher education worldwide by emphasizing excellence as the primary marketing strategy for attracting students, and by firmly resisting the temptation to lower standards in order to take advantage of new markets.

Reference List

Blight, Denis. 1997. "Factors Defining the Role of Academic Cooperation Agencies for the Internationalisation Process at the Turn of the Century." *Making the Case for International Cooperation in Higher Education: The Meise Consensus.* Conference proceedings prepared by the Academic Cooperation Association, Brussels, 45-51.

Bode, Christian. 1997. "What's New in Internationalisation." *Making the Case for International Cooperation in Higher Education: The Meise Consensus.* Conference proceedings prepared by the Academic Cooperation Association, Brussels, 41-45.

Davis, Todd M., ed. 1998. *Open Doors 1997–1998 Report on International Educational Exchange.* New York: Institute of International Education.

Kälvermark, Torsten, ed., 1997. *National Policies for the Internationalisation of Higher Education in Europe.* Stockholm: Hogskoleverket.

Kälvermark, Torsten, and Marijk van der Wende. 1997. "Conclusions and Discussion." In *National Policies for the Internationalisation of Higher Education in Europe,* Torsten Kälvermark, ed. Stockholm: Hogskoleverket, 259-71.

Rubin, Kyna. 1996. "Australia Takes Center Stage." *International Educator* 5, 4 (Summer): 26-30.

Background

1.1

International Recruitment in U.S. Higher Education — A Brief History

Stephen C. Dunnett

1.2

Ethics in International Student Recruitment

Linda Heaney

International Recruitment in U.S. Higher Education— A Brief History

AT MOST U.S. COLLEGES AND UNIVERSITIES, international recruitment has become a formal, standalone administrative endeavor only within the past 15 years, as competition for international students and the perceived benefits they offer to postsecondary institutions has markedly increased. Previously, relatively few institutions had any programs aimed at recruiting students from other countries. Those that did typically were private colleges that recruited international students to diversify their enrollment. Some private colleges affiliated with religious institutions for many years recruited students through missionary outposts in Africa, Asia, and Latin America.

The 1970s marked a turning point in the nature and scope of international recruitment activities undertaken by or on behalf of U.S. higher education institutions. This period marked not only the beginning of large-scale overseas recruitment efforts by many institutions, but also the proliferation of third-party recruiters who often charged a hefty fee to help foreign students— particularly those from oil-rich countries—gain admission to an American college or university.

During that decade, as the profitable business of third-party recruiting expanded, so did the likelihood of abuse. Unethical recruitment practices, incidences of gross misrepresentation of American higher education overseas, and violations of U.S. immigration laws led to growing criticism by students, parents, and officials overseas as well as by educators and the general public in the United States. The worsening situation led university administrators and professional associations to investigate recruitment practices and to develop ethical standards for international recruitment that would apply to institutions and their representatives abroad. NAFSA members played a major role in developing standards that served the interests of both international students and U.S. higher education.

The Emergence of International Recruitment As a Major Enterprise

Several factors accounted for the growth in the importance of international student recruitment in this period. The most obvious was the extraordinary increase in the number of foreign students seeking admission to U.S. institutions. In the 1960s and 1970s the number of self-funded foreign students grew dramatically worldwide, thanks largely to improvements in the economies and educational systems of many developing countries. Despite steep increases in real tuition charges at U.S. colleges and universities and decreases in financial aid from the federal government, international student enrollments increased rapidly—from 53,107 in 1960 to 336,990 in 1982. Even though the American share of the foreign student population worldwide declined during this period, the market for such students became increasingly important to U.S. institutions (Agarwal and Winkler 1985).

Although the pool of eligible students abroad expanded rapidly, demographic changes in the United States reduced domestic enrollments at many institutions. It was expected that after 1979 the number of American 18-year-olds would drop steadily until the mid-1990s, affecting all but a few colleges and universities. By the mid-1970s senior administrators and admission officers were responding to anticipated declines in enrollments of traditional college-age students and seeking ways to compensate for the shortfall.

The fall-off in the rate of growth of domestic enrollments occurred during an era of increasing fiscal austerity for many colleges and universities, which were therefore under growing pressure to maintain enrollments and boost tuition revenues. Many institutions closed, retrenched, or refashioned themselves to serve new markets. Aggressive recruitment programs were undertaken, and, as costs went up, financial aid awards also increased to ensure that students enrolled. Although enrollments increased again in the late 1970s, the enrollment prospects for the future were not encouraging. The number of postsecondary institutions in the United States kept rising, from 2,556 in 1970 to 3,231 in 1980 to more than 3,500 in 1990—making the competition for students even more fierce.

The one bright spot in the forecast was the projection that international student enrollments would continue to increase rapidly throughout the 1980s. It was expected that as domestic enrollments fell, colleges and universities would compete for and enroll larger numbers of international students. In a study commissioned by the Institute of International Education (IIE) in 1983, Goodwin and Nacht observed:

> The numbers [of foreign students coming to the United States] continued to increase through thick and thin, approximately doubling every decade. Nothing seemed to impede the flow—the end of Camelot, the Vietnam War, rising criticism of the role of

the United States in the world. . . . Even the United States' harshest foreign critics continued to send their youth to this country for higher education and were prepared to pay the mounting cost.

Seeing self-funded international students as one way to address enrollment problems, institutions began to look more seriously at overseas recruitment. In many cases the resulting recruitment activities did not serve the ultimate mission of the institutions nor were they in the best interest of the foreign students who were recruited. (As it happened, total enrollments in U.S. higher education increased between 1980 and 1990, but only by 4 percent, from 12 to 12.4 million.)

The goal of internationalizing U.S. higher education by "importing" foreign students was part of a larger vision articulated by some educators who called on colleges and universities to overcome their provincialism and adopt a global perspective. Their aims were to better prepare their students, to foster mutually beneficial exchanges and collaborative activities with partner institutions abroad, and ultimately to promote better cooperation and understanding between the United States and other countries.

Although they were less vulnerable to the demographic changes affecting undergraduate enrollment, research universities faced their own challenge. It became increasingly difficult in the 1980s to recruit enough qualified students into science and engineering graduate programs. To maintain these programs and to continue their extensive research endeavors, departments looked increasingly to international students to make up for the shortfall. Over time, international students came to dominate many graduate programs in these fields, in some cases representing 70 percent or more of the enrollment. Without them, many of these programs could not have been sustained.

Administrators of large universities took it for granted that ever-increasing numbers of international students would come to the United States without special recruitment efforts because of the appeal of American higher education: superior programs, faculty, and facilities; as well as openness, accessibility, and flexibility. This complacency would later be challenged as students in key markets such as Asia began to be recruited in larger numbers by institutions in other countries, notably Britain and Australia.

As the number of self-funded international students coming to the United States grew, the costs of higher education became an increasingly important factor in enrollment decisions and hence in recruitment strategies. Although it is not clear how many prospective international students were prevented from enrolling because of high costs, the proportion of those enrolling in public universities, where tuition is lower, clearly increased over time.

Foreign students generate revenues for colleges and universities by paying tuition and/or increasing state government subventions in the case of public institutions. . . . That so many colleges and universities enroll and even recruit foreign students suggests that, from the institutional perspective, there are real financial gains from such enrollments. (Agarwal and Winkler 1985)

Soon higher education was a leading American export, representing billion of dollars in revenue not only to colleges and universities but also to the localities in which international students resided.

Dealing with Abuses: The 1980 Wingspread Colloquium

In the late 1970s the financial benefit represented by increased numbers of self-funded international students, particularly those from oil-rich countries in the Middle East, proved an unfortunate temptation to some institutions badly hurt by falling domestic enrollments. The need to recruit more international students for the sake of revenue led in some cases to unethical recruitment practices.

Several high-level efforts to investigate recruitment practices and propose ethical standards for international recruitment were organized. The most important of these was the Wingspread Colloquium, held in March 1980, which addressed the topic "Foreign Student Recruitment: Realities and Recommendations." Sponsored by the National Liaison Committee on Foreign Student Admissions—a coalition made up of NAFSA, the American Association of Collegiate Registrars and Admissions Officers (AACRAO), IIE, the Council of Graduate Schools, and the College Board—the colloquium was attended by foreign students, admission officers, overseas educational advisers, foreign student advisers, and representatives of professional organizations, consortia, and government agencies.

The idea for the colloquium developed from concerns raised by NAFSA's Admissions Section (ADSEC). The stated purpose of the colloquium was in part:

> [T]o examine the demographic and economic conditions which have created the need to increase recruiting practices, the activities—good and bad—currently taking place, including a review of the agents in the recruitment business, and the alternatives facing the U.S. educational community in responding to fast-growing, increasingly uncontrolled, and ethically suspect activities.

In addition, the participants sought "to formulate recommendations toward centralizing information on recruitment practices and tightening standards in the identification of appropriate students from overseas and the processing of their admission to United States institutions" (Jenkins 1980).

The more immediate impetus behind the colloquium was several egregious and highly publicized cases of unethical recruitment by U.S. institutions. One notorious example that drew considerable media and public attention involved Windham College, which recruited and enrolled foreign students who discovered upon arriving on campus that the college had closed as a result of financial problems (Jenkins 1980).

Although the colloquium focused chiefly on the problems associated with the recruitment and admission of foreign students, it did not recommend a reduction in the flow of students coming to the United States from abroad. Rather, it called for more responsible and effective oversight of the process of directing students to suitable U.S. institutions, a curb on the abuses, and the promotion of professional and institutional standards for ethical recruitment.

As a result of the discussions of the two working groups in the colloquium, it was agreed that (1) a clearinghouse of information on international recruitment should be established and endorsed by the major educational associations, and (2) a set of criteria should be put forward as a basis for promoting ethical recruitment practices. These criteria stipulated that institutions should provide prospective international students with accurate and adequate information about the institutions, their programs, costs, and support services, and about U.S. higher education in general, to enable the students to make well-informed decisions when seeking admission.

In addition, the criteria called for the establishment of effective institutional policies on foreign-student recruitment, admissions, and support services, and advocated restricting the evaluation of foreign academic credentials to suitably qualified admission professionals. In addressing the controversial practice of paying agents for each student recruited, the colloquium recommended that institutions "avoid contractual arrangements with agents who require fee-for-enrollment payments."

The recommendations of the Wingspread Colloquium formed the basis for NAFSA's "Guidelines for Ethical Recruitment," incorporated into NAFSA's "Principles for International Educational Exchange" (appendix A) and "Code of Ethics" (appendix B).

Recent Developments: Tours, Fairs, and "Enrollment Management"

Some forward-looking U.S. colleges and universities began formal recruitment and international student scholarship programs in the 1970s. In the late 1970s and early 1980s IIE sponsored educational tours to multiple Asian countries for university administrators. The purpose of the IIE program was to help the administrators learn more about Asian educational systems and at the same time provide an opportunity for Asian students to get some first-hand information from U.S. college administrators. Those tours laid the foundation for future group travel in Asia.

When international enrollments first began to level off in the mid-1980s and competition for international students grew more intense, more and more admission offices began employing in the international market recruitment techniques that had been developed to recruit domestic students. Indeed, some methods had been used much earlier in the history of U.S. higher education. Admission staff created promotional publications and other admission materials specifically for international students, participated in the growing number of university fairs, established extensive contacts with a network of local schools and overseas educational advisers, enlisted the help of faculty and alumni in foreign countries to meet with prospective students, and developed sophisticated databases and tracking systems to ensure better oversight of the admission process from initial contact to enrollment.

Overseas recruitment tours to university fairs, schools, and educational advising centers have become an essential component of international recruitment programs. In 1972 the European Council of International Schools (ECIS) conducted the first recruitment tour of Europe for U.S. colleges and universities. The purpose of the tour, which involved some fifteen U.S. institutions, was to make it possible for students in international schools in Europe to meet directly with U.S. admission representatives. Similarly, in 1982 the College Information Exchange organized a tour to Latin America at the request of guidance counselors in Central and South America who wanted their students to have direct access to U.S. admission officers. That was also the year in which Linden Educational Services first conducted a recruitment tour of Asia, and IIE discontinued its educational tours for university administrators.

In the 1980s and early 1990s many campuses set up centralized offices of "enrollment management," headed by senior administrators often at the vice-presidential level. Originating as an extension of the admission office, enrollment management came to encompass many other areas, including retention, financial aid, student services, and academic advisement (Dixon 1995). Consequently, international recruitment came to be viewed as an integral part of a comprehensive enrollment management plan.

More recently, international recruitment has been facilitated by the development of information technologies that have made possible not only instant communication by fax, e-mail, and the Internet with students in remote locations, but also greater efficiencies in the admission process. In particular, the World Wide Web has become an invaluable recruitment tool, allowing ready access for many students overseas to a broad range of up-to-date campus information and contacts, as well as online application materials.

As the number of international applicants has grown, so have the complexities involved in evaluating foreign credentials and awarding transfer credit for courses completed at overseas institutions. International recruitment of graduate and professional students poses special challenges because graduate applicants lie outside the networks of contacts among universities and econdary school counselors and faculty. As a result, U.S. graduate recruiters must develop their own contacts with faculty in undergraduate programs abroad who might refer qualified applicants.

In the 1990s international student recruitment became a big business, with a variety of consultants, professional organizations, and for-profit companies providing a wide range of services, both in the United States and abroad, to colleges and universities. These services included professional development workshops; marketing and enrollment-management consultancy; organized recruitment tours to different countries and regions; advising and referral services; credentials evaluation services; advertising and publicity in print, video, and electronic media; and hardware and software development to facilitate admissions and enrollment management functions. As they developed more organized and systematic international recruitment programs, colleges and universities were better able to track and manage their international enrollments to meet their institutional objectives.

The 1990s also were an era of fiscal austerity and retrenchment, especially for public institutions, which in some cases have looked to higher tuition charged to international students as a vital revenue stream. Demographic projections indicate that the number of 18-year-olds in the United States, which declined between 1985 and 1995, will not recover for another decade, particularly in regions such as the Northeast (Baer and Stace 1997). As the number of international students in U.S. postsecondary education leveled off around 450,000 in the mid-1990s, competition for students heated up, recruitment activities became even more aggressive, and enrollment managers scrambled to keep up with the changing circumstances.

The financial crisis that struck East and Southeast Asia in the mid- to late-1990s came as a rude awakening to institutions that had become dependent on enrollments of Asian students. For much of the previous two decades, between 50 and 60 percent of all international students in U.S. postsecondary education had come from Asia. In 1996–97, according to *Open Doors,* the annual census of international student flows to and from the United States, Canada was the only non-Asian country on the list of the top ten countries of origin. Many intensive English programs were particularly reliant on Asian students and therefore more vulnerable to the crisis.

The situation in Asia demonstrated once again the fluidity of the international student market and the imprudence of depending too much on enrollments of students from one country or region. This lesson had already been learned by those colleges and universities that had enrolled large numbers of students from the Middle East in the late 1970s and early 1980s, before the Iranian revolution of 1979–80 and falling oil prices reduced their number from approximately 85,000 in 1980 to fewer than 50,000 five years later.

The crisis in Asia reminded institutions to diversify their overseas recruitment efforts to include other promising markets such as Latin America,

Central and Eastern Europe, Russia, Eurasia, Turkey, and India. Even before the financial difficulties in Asia, educators at many U.S. colleges and universities saw the need to diversify their enrollments in order to achieve a better mix of students on campus, to afford their international students and all students a more satisfying educational experience, and to ensure better retention and graduation rates.

Reference List

Agarwal, Vinod B., and Donald R. Winkler. 1985. "Migration of Foreign Students to the United States." *Journal of Higher Education* 56, 5: 509–522.

Baer, Michael A., and Peter A. Stace. 1997. "Enrollment Management." In *First Among Equals: The Role of the Chief Academic Officer,* ed. James Martin et al. Baltimore: Johns Hopkins University Press.

Dixon, Rebecca R. 1995. "What Is Enrollment Management?" In *Making Enrollment Management Work,* ed. Rebecca R. Dixon. San Francisco: Jossey-Bass.

Goodwin, Craufurd D., and Michael Nacht. 1983. *Absence of Decision: Foreign Students in American Colleges and Universities.* New York: Institute of International Education.

Jenkins, Hugh M. 1980. *Foreign Student Recruitment: Realities and Recommendations.* New York: College Board.

NAFSA: Association of International Educators. 1993. *Standards and Policies in International Educational Exchange.* Washington, DC: NAFSA.

Ethics in International Student Recruitment

LIKE DOMESTIC ADMISSION, international student recruitment is grounded in a set of well-understood principles. It begins with a commitment from the institution, often noted in its mission statement, to value international students and their contributions to the student body and to provide them with the programs and services they need to succeed.

The recruitment process requires constant vigilance, because abuses have taken place and will most likely continue to occur, albeit in very small numbers. The root cause is ignorance or naiveté—of foreign students who are vulnerable to misinformation, of administrators looking for easy answers to difficult enrollment questions, of admission representatives insufficiently trained in evaluating international credentials, and of representatives of the institution not familiar with the NAFSA's Code of Ethics.

NAFSA's Principles and Code

NAFSA first addressed unprofessional recruiting practices at the Wingspread Colloquium in March 1980. Criteria for ethical recruitment were developed, which later became part of NAFSA's "Principles for International Educational Exchange" (appendix A). This strong, thoughtful, policy-oriented document articulates a rationale for exchanges, and supports the policy statements with a program of institutional self-regulation. The self-regulation program was designed to help institutions recognize what they needed to offer international students.

From 1981 to 1989, NAFSA considered how a program of self-regulation might be developed, administered, and enforced. The association's goal was to have (1) a formal set of standards, (2) training for its members about the standards, and (3) a mechanism for enforcing the standards. In 1989, NAFSA's board of directors adopted NAFSA's Code of Ethics. Sections 7 and 8 of the code address the responsibilities of admission officers and individuals with responsibility for teaching English as a second language. The code is reprinted in appendix B and is available on NAFSA's web site.

In addition to these sections, the code also outlines the responsibilities of members in their relationships with students, scholars, and other professionals, and offers guidelines in the areas of program administration, public statements, student advising, study abroad, and community relations.

NAFSA's Committee on Ethical Practice promotes the code and handles allegations of violations. An average of three complaints reach the committee each year. With the assistance of the NAFSA staff, complainants are encouraged to resolve the issue before involving the committee. If the problem is not resolved, the committee will review the complaint for relevance to the code and render an opinion to the complainant. Reprimand, censure, and suspension from membership can occur after a lengthy, careful, and complete investigation.

Federal Regulations

Recruitment abuses first became known to the public through the misuse of official forms used to obtain student visas. University officials should have a basic understanding of federal regulations governing the issuance of the Certificate of Eligibility (Form I-20) and the requirements set forth for a student visa. Briefly, an applicant for a student visa must (1) have a bona fide offer of admission and show intent to register as a full-time student, (2) be capable of paying tuition, fees, health insurance, and living expenses, and (3) have no intention of permanently abandoning his or her place of legal residence. The pertinent regulations, with analysis and guidance, may be found in the *Adviser's Manual of Federal Regulations Affecting Foreign Students and Scholars* (Washington, DC: NAFSA, 1998).

The National Association for College Admission Counseling's (NACAC) "Guidelines for the Recruitment, Admission, and Support of International Students" also specify good practices for colleges and universities to follow. NACAC's guidelines are reprinted as appendix C.

Challenges in the Recruitment of International Students

Pressure on institutions to increase enrollments and generate revenues, coupled with demands from alumni, donors, and board members to foster a more global outlook on campus, give rise to several challenges.

The Imperative of Providing Complete and Accurate Information

International students not only need complete, accurate, and current information, but also a context in which to place that information. Institutions should be clear about what they are offering international applicants. Consider, for example, an international student admitted to a pre-engineering program. The student should be informed that transfer to an engineering school may be required after two or three years of pre-engineering study, that transfer may not be automatic, and that procedures will need to be followed to complete the transfer. If credit is given for previous studies, students should be informed about how many of these credits count toward the degree, and whether the student will have to meet a residency requirement to obtain the degree.

Providing a context for information is particularly important in matters relating to costs and financial assistance. Students who hear about the minimum wage in the United States often think they can live on this amount if they can get 20 hours of work a week. They also think they can live miles from the campus and rely on public transportation. Because most international students cannot fathom the costs relating to health care, most do not understand the necessity of having health insurance. Students need a context in which to put the numbers.

Placement Agency

A placement agency approaches a college international admission officer regarding prospective students from China. The agency is eager to place Chinese students at the college, but the students can't afford the costs stated on the promotional materials. Since Chinese students tend to live off-campus in groups of three or four and eat very inexpensively, the agency representative argues, the college should accept verification of a lower figure for these students and issue Forms I-20 accordingly. The admission officer, upon reviewing subsequent applications from the agency, finds its students to be academically and linguistically qualified. He accepts the students and issues the Forms I-20, listing a standard of financial resources $1,500 lower than that listed for all other international students. (NAFSA's Committee on Ethical Practice, 1998)

NAFSA's Committee on Ethical Practice believes that this practice is a violation of NAFSA's Code of Ethics. The applicable provisions of NAFSA's Code of Ethics are 1(b) and (c); 3(h); 5(a); 6(b); 7(b)(5) and (d). The committee urges members to "maintain a high level of professional conduct and keep the needs of the student in balance with the needs of the institution." By lowering the support figure the official designated to sign I-20s puts his or her job and institution at risk with the Immigration and Naturalization Service (INS) and does a great disservice to students. The naive official may also be jeopardizing his institution's privilege to issue I-20s if this practice is observed by the INS. Students need to understand that the costs given are the same as those U.S. students might pay for housing, food, health care, and incidental expenses. In addition, international students will need funds for holiday and vacation periods.

Institutions have a responsibility to provide accurate and realistic cost information to all applicants. Official university cost estimates should be used for all students, domestic or international, for all official university transactions. Some countries have foreign exchange controls and will allow students to take out of the country only the amount listed on the official forms. If a student chooses to live in other housing, he or she needs the same resources as the other enrolled students. See *Basic F-1 Procedures for Beginners,* ed. Masume Assaf and Linda Gentile (Washington, DC: NAFSA, 1998).

Scholarships and Financial Aid

Millions of prospective international students are unable to bear the high cost of studying in the United States. They need to know if the institutions they are considering can offer them enough financial assistance to realistically cover their expenses. They need to know if this assistance will be available for the duration of their studies and how to apply for it.

> An international student writes to a university requesting application forms. In his letter he indicates that he requires full financial assistance. The university sends back its standard response letter and application forms. It does not address the student's financial concerns. The university offers a few partial scholarships but no full ones.

It is the university's responsibility to provide complete and accurate information about financial support opportunities in order to give students the basis for an informed choice. When prospective applicants indicate that they are going to need full financial assistance but receive application forms and literature that omit this important policy information, students frequently assume financial aid is available. They then spend time and money applying to a school they cannot afford to attend.

University letters or brochures should detail the international student scholarship and financial aid policies (and any other policies that might affect international students' transition to U.S. higher education) so there is no confusion about whether a student can afford a particular college. International student correspondence should be read carefully and answered helpfully.

Third-Party Representation of Students

Sometimes abuse occurs when students use consultants and agencies to help them find a place in a university. In many countries, it is customary to use a go-between to accomplish difficult tasks, but the agent may not be familiar with U.S. university admission policies, procedures, and practices. Difficulties may arise if the student is not fluent in English or if the agent assumes too much authority while trying to assist the student. Under such circumstances, universities should take precautions by assuming direct correspondence with the student once the referral has been made. This includes having the applicant sign the application himself, verifying all transcripts with the institution that issued the document, and making clear to the student all the costs of attending the U.S. institution. (See also chapter 4.4, Working with Third-Party Recruiters and Agents.)

> An organization with a prestigious-sounding name approaches a university seeking to place a group of students. It says it comes with the blessing of the embassy and wants the admission officer to offer blanket approval to all of the students in the group.

Universities should follow the same admission practices for international students that they follow for domestic students, which means reviewing the applications one at a time. It is often true that borderline students require disproportionate time and attention from the faculty, international student services staff, and others on campus. Unqualified students cannot make effective contributions to the campus, and frustrate faculty and fellow students alike. No one benefits from their admission.

Admission officers should be friendly and open with representatives, but in the course of the communication, ask for information about the organization and its business experience. If necessary, verify the relationship with the embassy and the embassy's interest in this student placement. At the same time, make clear to the representative that the university never allows others to make its admission decisions, and that their students will have to apply in the same way other students do. You may offer to expedite the processing of the applications if you think considering a group all at once will be an advantage for your enrollment program.

On-the-Spot Admission

Because British and Australian universities have stepped up their recruitment efforts and now offer "on-the-spot" admission, more students are demanding immediate rulings on admission decisions. U.S. government regulations require that admission decisions be made at the institution's U.S. location, and that the university obtain a written application, the student's transcript and other records of courses taken, proof of adequate financial resources, and other supporting documents before making the decision. NAFSA recommends that admission judgments be made by institutional personnel who rule on other admissions, based on a system of written criteria and applied in competition with other applicants.

> An international admission officer makes annual recruitment trips, working with local agencies in each of the countries she visits. Upon reading her advertisements in the local newspaper, prospective students flock to see her, academic credentials in hand. The admission officer assesses English proficiency through personal conversations with these individuals and, provided they meet academic and financial requirements, offers them admission on the spot.
> (NAFSA's Committee on Ethical Practice, 1998)

This method of admitting students violates NAFSA's Code of Ethics. Applicable provisions of the code are 1(a); 2(a) and (b), and 8(a). Furthermore, U.S. government regulations prohibit such behavior, requiring that international admission decisions be made at the "school's location in the United States" (8 Code of Federal Regulations 214.2(k)(2)). Most admission officers, knowledgeable about their school's criteria, will give the student a realistic assessment of admission and inform the student about when he or she can expect a decision from the institution.

Proactive, Ethical Recruitment

Some suggestions for those responsible for international student recruitment follow. Teaching, nudging, reminding, and monitoring others on campus about the importance of giving students complete and accurate information are common themes.

- Know that ethical behavior and standards are a part of your job.

- Recognize that if ethical standards are maintained, both the student and the institution will benefit.

- Educate your colleagues and senior administration about the need for maintaining ethical standards, and about NAFSA's Code of Ethics. One of the best ways to do this is to keep your administration aware of changes in the international student market so they can be prepared for changing enrollments. Ethical standards are tested when enrollment targets are not being met.

- Monitor closely the work of alumni and others who represent your institution.

- Review your written materials to see that they portray your institution accurately.

- Think about how much time must be devoted to borderline or failing students and make every effort to admit only those students who meet your admission criteria.

- Understand the difference between a placement agency that works on behalf of the student and an agency that recruits for your institution. Individuals who do both will, sooner or later, make a less-than-perfect match.

- Require that agencies that represent you become thoroughly familiar with your institution and the students it educates. Limit the scope of what the agent can and cannot do for your institution.

- Hold meetings at least annually between decision-makers and those who actively recruit overseas to assess results, discuss lessons learned, and make future plans.

The winning combination is a student who thoughtfully chooses to enroll in an institution knowing that he is well-qualified and excited about the course offerings and campus environment, and an institution that proudly graduates a student from another country. This can only happen when international student recruiters do their job well and maintain the highest of standards. NAFSA's Code of Ethics is a blueprint for admission representatives as they plan and implement their recruitment efforts. It should be used by admission representatives and shared with the wider university community.

Preparing to Recruit

Preparing to Recruit

AS WITH MANY THINGS IN LIFE, laying the proper groundwork can make the difference between success and failure. The same is true of recruiting international students. The institution that approaches recruiting with a clear understanding of its reasons for doing so, with articulated goals and outcomes, and with the commitment to provide infrastructure for the increased number of students on campus will stand a much better chance of success than the organization that approaches this task naively, haphazardly, or without campus-wide consensus.

Foundations for Recruiting

The reasons for recruiting international students should be grounded in the institution's mission. A private institution that offers a liberal arts education will draw upon a different pool of students than a community college or vocational institute, whose reasons for existence may be to teach pragmatic skills with immediate application in the workplace. Likewise, a large research institution may attempt to attract students to fill its teaching or basic research needs, freeing the faculty to do more advanced work.

It is important to recognize and emphasize your institution's strengths when recruiting international students. This may include (1) identifying academic programs that enjoy particular popularity among domestic students or a reputation for excellence among peer institutions; (2) discovering faculty with particularly rich international experience (and, one hopes, empathy for international perspectives) or areas of expertise that are in particular demand; and (3) highlighting facilities that exceed the norm in their innovative design or educational capacity (recent capital improvement projects on campus are a good place to begin).

Other infrastructural elements that can be explored when seeking support for recruiting include existing institutional programs and initiatives, such as language and area studies (whose faculty presumably have a vested interest in hosting students from other countries), development projects, formal and informal linkages with overseas institutions, faculty exchange agreements, and study-abroad programs.

Try to concentrate your recruiting efforts on areas of your school's endeavors that are already vibrant, attractive, and in demand, or on areas that have traditionally supported international educational exchange.

Risks and Benefits

The rewards of recruiting international students are obvious to those committed to international educational exchange. International students provide opportunities for culture-sharing and may complement a school's diversity goals. Generally, international students are well-prepared and well-motivated for a course of study in the United States. And, of course, international students' educational experiences at your school will remain in their memories the rest of their lives. They will become proponents of U.S. higher education and particularly of your institution, assuming their experience at your school was positive.

On the other hand, enrolling international students may entail risk. Not all students from abroad are exceptionally prepared for academic study in the United States, and some may require remedial coursework in academic areas or English, or experience financial difficulty while enrolled.

International students require different support services than their American counterparts. An out-of-state student doesn't need a visa to visit home and return, nor does she need your help acquiring work authorization to undertake an academic internship or get permission for an academically related summer job.

Perhaps your goal is to increase interaction between U.S. and international students. Proximity does not necessarily result in empathy or understanding. Is your institution committed to the extra staffing that may be required to facilitate structured, positive intercultural experiences among the student body? What if your international recruits don't want to participate? What will you do if they form isolated cliques based on national origins, or if they are critical of the host culture?

Emphasizing an institution's strengths can result in an oversubscription of students in courses or majors in high demand. When we admit students from other countries, we are obligated to ensure that there are enough seats available for them to fulfill the goals for which they came to the United States.

Another area of concern is the political and economic volatility of the international community. The political and economic ties among countries are becoming tighter and the social and economic ties more entangled. International students may face disruptions in funding from their home countries, resulting in cash-flow problems at the host institution in the United States. Military posturing or outright conflict among nations may not only disrupt foreign currency exchange, but may also result in tensions among student groups on campuses, and panic, depression, and psychosomatic illnesses in affected populations. Policies promulgated by U.S. government agencies, such as the Immigration and Naturalization Service (INS), the Department of State, and the Department of Labor, have a direct impact on the quality of an international student's educational experience in the United States. International students' perceptions of the United States are created by more than television and Hollywood. Ask anyone who was treated rudely at a port of entry or whose spouse was denied a dependent visa for incomprehensible reasons if he is inclined to send his children to study in the United States.

Figure 2.1-1 outlines the benefits and risks of enrolling international students.

FIGURE 2.1-1
BENEFITS AND RISKS OF ENROLLING INTERNATIONAL STUDENTS

BENEFITS	RISKS
• International students enhance the educational environment of the institution. Most are superior students who are highly motivated.	• The ability of higher education to adapt to new levels of demand may be impeded; at the undergraduate level, international students tend to enroll in high-demand courses.
• International students may keep underenrolled graduate classes or whole departments operational.	
• International students enrich the cultural climate of the campus and increase the diversity of the student body.	• Large numbers of students from one country may cluster and fail to mix with others on campus or in the community.
• Increasing numbers of international students means more tuition and fee income for the institution.	• International students require special services, may enroll in high-cost courses, and may have cash-flow problems.
• A recognized international dimension is a plus for fundraising.	
• International students may become "friends in high places" for the institution, the state, and the United States.	• Perceived problems with international students can affect institutional prestige.
• International students may not be fully equipped linguistically or academically to function in the U.S. educational system.	• International students may return home with a negative image of the United States, or they may remain in the United States illegally.

Source: Adapted from Mary Peterson, "What's the Key to Success in Recruiting International Students?" *The Admission Strategist*, Fall 1994: 7.

Readiness to Recruit

Is your institution ready to recruit and retain international students? After you have clarified your school's motivations for recruiting students and decided that it's time to develop a recruitment plan, a preliminary inventory of policies and resources is in order. For example, current admission standards for academic performance and English proficiency should be examined and consensus reached about admission requirements. Perhaps admission staff members have regional or country-specific expertise in foreign credentials evaluations. Is it wise to focus only upon this student pool in your international recruitment efforts? Like a stock portfolio designed to achieve growth over a long period of time, an effective recruitment strategy will diversify its pool of students in order to minimize the risks associated with regional political disruptions or economic downturns.

Another litmus test of recruitment readiness is the institution's willingness to devote resources to the effort. Increasing your school's profile in the global marketplace will require a substantial investment in publications, mailing expenses, technology, and personnel. Creating a niche in the international student market may require a recruiter with some linguistic expertise and regional contacts, admission counselors with broad experience, and an increase in student service staffing. With growth comes complexity, and it is unwise to expect current personnel levels to be able to address the needs of the new campus environment that will be created by the presence of more international students.

Finally, it's not enough to bring new students to campus. They must persist and succeed in their educational goals for maximum benefits to accrue. Retention rates are reinforced by an institutional culture that values the presence of international students. This will be reflected in the level of support services devoted to international students, including special programming designed either to address the unique needs of such students or to mainstream them into the general student population (where, after all, they will do the most to "internationalize" your school).

Campus and Community Services

The following inventory of campus and community services may serve as a preliminary checklist for schools considering international student recruitment. International students will impact many other campus services, but these, at minimum, must be in place.

Admission. A school's admission office plays a central role in any student recruitment effort. Its responsibilities may include participating in policy decisions (e.g., setting standards for admission); planning and conducting recruitment trips; developing, printing, and mailing application materials; advising prospective students and applicants; processing and evaluating applications for admission; providing orientation for new students; and conducting research relating to the recruitment, admission, and retention of students.

- Will additional staff be needed to respond to application requests from abroad? What is an acceptable turnaround time for applications? Will it be necessary to employ such staff year-round, or will the demands be seasonal?

- Will additional staff be needed to process and evaluate applications in a timely manner?

- Will the admission office be in a position to deal with requests from academic departments for more detailed information on students' educational backgrounds for purposes of admission and advising?

- Has your school developed an application form targeted at international students? If so, is the form adequate? Your office may face a deluge of inquiries if the form does not address the needs and concerns of its target audience.

- Are your publications competitive? Print is only one way of reaching potential students. Does your school have a recruiting video or CD-ROM designed for international students? Does your international admission office have a presence on the World Wide Web?

- Should you consider developing country-specific application and recruiting materials?

- Will the admission office need to expand its library of materials on the educational systems of other countries? These references might include books, newsletters, periodicals, electronic resources, and information gained from professional conferences. Is there a budget for such things?

Scholarships and Financial Aid. Schools interested in recruiting international students may consider offering financial aid incentives to attract high-quality applicants. In addition to direct aid from institutional sources, other forms of student assistance can be explored. International students are not eligible for federal financial aid, and employment opportunities are limited by immigration regulations.

- Should the prospect of financial aid be used to support the recruiting of international students? If so, who will supply the funding? Will the scholarships be awarded on the basis of merit or need? Especially in regard to the latter, how can applicants be judged?

- Is there an adequate supply of on-campus jobs from which international students might earn some spending money and contribute to payment of their expenses? Are graduate assistantships available, and do they pay a high enough salary to support a single student's education?

- Is there an emergency loan fund or source of emergency grants for students who experience unanticipated financial difficulty? If not, can such a fund be created? If so, will the program grow to accommodate an inevitable increase in applicants?

English As a Second Language.   Many colleges and universities offer several levels of English as a second language (ESL) programs, from conventional "intensive" study programs for non-degree-seeking students to remedial coursework for degree-seeking students and special programs to certify graduate teaching assistants' English-language proficiency levels.

- Can a way be found to predict accurately the number of new students who will need to be tested for placement in these programs?

- Will there be provision for adequate space and staff for testing new students?

- Will there be funds to increase the number of ESL sections offered in proportion to any increase in enrollment? Will there be adequate faculty, course offerings, and course levels?

- Will additional clerical support be available for an enlarged ESL program?

- Should intensive English students be allowed to take some academic coursework before completing their course of English study? What level of proficiency will qualify them for concurrent academic coursework?

- If you have no plans to offer ESL assistance, is such assistance readily available in your community, perhaps at another institution with which you may be able to form a partnership?

- Will an adequate number of remedial ESL courses be offered for students whose academic performance would be compromised without additional ESL work?

- Will academic support and remedial services include assistance in writing, conversational English, and reading?

Academic Advising and Course Placement.   Academic advising and course placement services are critical to new international students, most of whom are unfamiliar with the U.S. academic system. Availability of these services will make a huge difference, not only in the students' academic success or failure, but also in their general cultural adjustment.

- Will advisers be on duty during the weeks or days before the beginning of classes to advise new international students?

- If academic advising is centralized at the undergraduate level or within graduate departments, will there be enough academic advising staff to accommodate an increased population of international students?

- Will such staff have some familiarity with foreign credentials, so that proper course placement is assured?

- Are academic advisers comfortable talking with people from other countries, or is some cross-cultural communication training in order?

- Will advisers have the ability to track student progress and make mid-course corrections in curricular selections during the student's program?

- Will an increase in international students be mirrored by an increase in course availability, especially in those majors that attract large numbers of students?

Housing. Housing issues can be divided into on-campus and off-campus concerns. The degree to which either is predominant will depend on the type of institution (e.g., commuter, small private college with residence hall residency requirements, large institution) and the size of the community in which it is located (small town with limited off-campus housing vs. city with ample off-campus housing within commuting distance).

- What temporary housing, if any, will the school offer newly arrived international students as they seek off-campus housing or wait for on-campus housing contracts to begin?

- Should an international residence hall (or an international wing or floor) be established in an effort to recruit international students to the school and into the residence hall system?

- Should a segment of a residence hall be set aside for upper division or graduate students to make residence-hall living more appealing to them?

- Will residence-hall staff, particularly resident assistants who live on the floors, be given adequate training to deal with cross-cultural misunderstanding and conflict that may arise between American and international roommates?

- Will residence halls provide programming designed to increase understanding of cross-cultural issues?

- If there is family housing available on the campus, is there a community center for educational and social activities that would encourage interactions between international and U.S. families?

- Will students interested in living off-campus be provided assistance in looking for suitable housing?

- Does the school or the community sponsor a tenant-landlord association that can recommend standards of housing, legal wording in leases, and dispute resolution in cases of disagreement or misunderstanding?

Career Services and Placement. As competition for international students intensifies, it becomes increasingly important that students believe they are receiving a good return on their investment. For many, the most concrete result of their U.S. education may be employment after graduation.

- Does the placement office at your college serve the needs of international students? For example, is there timely information about opportunities abroad?

- Does the staff target international students in mailings or newsletters?

- Are placement counselors informed about federal regulations affecting employment in the United States for students from abroad?

- Does the international office meet routinely with the placement office to exchange information and discuss concerns?

Needs of Dependents. The demographics of higher education are changing. Adults are returning to college (or attending for the first time), and they often have dependents. International students are no different, especially at larger research institutions, which may attract professionals and government officials who are retooling in anticipation of mid-career changes or added responsibilities, postdoctoral students seeking additional research experience in the United States before accepting academic positions in their home countries, or people who have not postponed marriage and family before participating in international educational exchange.

Many spouses of international students are women of child-rearing age. The spouse may or may not have some English proficiency before arriving in the United States. Most dependents of international students are not able to work legally (the exception being dependents in J-2 status). With limited or no knowledge of the language, no opportunity to participate in the community through employment, and frequently shouldering primary child care responsibilities, the spouses of international students are even more vulnerable than their student spouses to isolation and culture shock.

- Will affordable, temporary housing be available while families search for appropriate permanent housing?

- Is inexpensive or free ESL instruction available for spouses who may need it to manage day-to-day household duties?

Does your community have enough day care facilities to support a sudden influx of children from other countries? Is it affordable for students, who frequently live at or near the poverty line?

Does the international office (or some other entity) sponsor an organization or activities for international student spouses, helping them integrate into the campus and community, and offering social support and practical assistance?

Are community social services prepared for an influx of foreign dependents? For example, will private healthcare providers be in a position to respond adequately to patients with different cultural values, illnesses not normally encountered in your part of the world, and (perhaps) limited English proficiency? Are the various levels of health and human service associations briefed as to the eligibility requirements for access to their services (e.g., WIC, Medicaid, food stamps)? Is a female physician practicing in the community?

Can the local schools accommodate students from other countries? Does the school district offer ESL instruction? Do administrators know how the Illegal Immigration Reform and Immigrant Responsibility Act of 1996 affects the nonimmigrants who enroll in their schools?

Health Care and Insurance.   International students are frequently baffled by the U.S. healthcare system because they often come from countries whose governments subsidize health care and insurance. There may be resentment toward campus policies that mandate insurance coverage or health screenings. Furthermore, the clinical paradigm learned at U.S. medical schools may confuse or offend international students. U.S. medical personnel may perform different roles than medical personnel in an international student's home country.

- How will campus or community health service staff become sensitized to cross-cultural health issues?

- Will your school require any mandatory screening of international students (e.g., for tuberculosis, for hepatitis-B)? If so, how will the requirement be justified to new students? Will the health center commit more resources to staffing in order to implement the requirements? How will this be funded?

- If your campus has a counseling service, is it prepared for a possible influx of new students experiencing adjustment difficulties? Are staff trained to recognize and treat depression and other psychological conditions that might be manifested by students from other cultures?

- Will health insurance be mandatory for international students? If so, how will the requirement be justified and explained? How will it be enforced?

Will students with dependents be required to purchase insurance for their dependents as well? If so, how will that requirement be enforced?

- If more international students enroll at your institution, what will be the impact on broader health services in the community? Will free, walk-in clinics see an increase in international patients (either students or their dependents)? Will emergency treatment centers become de facto ambulatory clinics for international students or their dependents?

International Student Services. The international student services office traditionally coordinates activities related to international exchange after students are admitted and arrive in the United States. The philosophical stance such an office takes toward its clients can have a huge impact on the success or failure of recruiting efforts. Some offices view themselves as deputized branches of the INS. These offices may concentrate extra resources on tracking students in an effort to uncover illegal activities. Other offices concentrate their resources on enhancing the academic experience of international students on campus and making their stay as comfortable and productive as possible.

Staffing needs in the international student services office will depend not only on the philosophical stance that office takes toward its clients, but also on the clients themselves. The volume and nature of the international student services office's work will vary with the size and composition of the international student population and in response to unpredictable world events.

- Will staffing be adequate to meet the anticipated demands of an increased international student population?

- What role will the international student services office play in the development of needed services for an influx of students? Will the office attempt to provide such services, or will the office attempt to "mainstream" students by coordinating services with existing campus units?

- What programming will the international student services office offer? Will there be orientation for new students upon arrival? Will there be ongoing programming designed to facilitate cross-cultural learning? Will there be co-curricular programming that integrates international students into the campus community and recognizes them as a valuable learning resource?

- Will the international student advising staff initiate campus-wide training programs to sensitize U.S. staff to the needs and concerns of international students and thereby create a more understanding environment? Will such training address cross-cultural communication skills and dispute mediation?

- How will the international student services office cope with the added amount of immigration advising that an increase in students will bring? Can the issuance of forms and documents be automated? Is there adequate staff to meet the demands of student travel, occasional visa difficulties, practical training applications, and other INS paperwork?

Recruiting international students can transform a campus for better or worse, depending upon many factors, including the preparedness of the campus or the increase in services this new population requires. Ill-conceived ventures may result in a sudden increase in tuition revenues in the short term, but campus fractionalization, hostility, and unhappiness in the long term. A more successful approach to growth will anticipate the educational needs and social support systems that international students require and will devote resources to building campus infrastructure to address those needs.

INTERNATIONAL STUDENT RECRUITMENT is more likely to succeed if it is done as a result of strategic planning rather than spontaneously or sporadically as a response to enrollment pressures. A strategic plan for international recruitment should be tied to the institution's overall plan for international student education. Ideally, it ought to be a component of a plan for the internationalization of the institution, which would encompass sending domestic students abroad, faculty and staff exchanges, and interinstitutional affiliations. At a minimum, it ought to be linked to the larger admission plan of the institution.

Much has been published about strategic planning and education, including myriad models and frameworks. Traditional mission-based models coexist with more recent models based on performance and outcomes, which are often used for enrollment management activities. The mission-based model derives from business; the performance-based method from the notion that higher education may benefit from a different focus in strategic planning, namely developing niches. A good discussion of performance-based strategic planning as "a formal process designed to help an organization identify and maintain an optimal alignment with the most important elements of its environment" can be found in *Working Toward Strategic Change* (Dolence, Rowley, and Lujan 1997).

If a strategic planning model is already in use at your institution, adopt it, because it is difficult to impose one system upon another. If there is no model, identify the method that will work best at your institution. This chapter addresses components of both mission-based and performance-based models. Most current strategic planning is mission based; the other, however, seems well tuned to recruitment and enrollment planning. Your institution will have to determine an optimal strategy: staying with a time-tested model, blending models, or switching to one that best suits its type and vision.

Key Elements in Strategic Planning

The following are crucial elements of strategic planning:

- Analysis and assessment of the external and internal environments

- Analysis of strengths, weaknesses, opportunities, and threats (SWOT analysis)

Development of mission and goals

• Identification of key performance indicators or measures of essential outcome

• Identification of objectives and an action plan

• Identification of resources, needs, and expenditures
(Dolence, Rowley, and Lujan 1997; Uhl 1983)

An effective strategic plan provides a framework for strategic thinking, direction, and action leading to the achievement of consistent and planned results. It should be tailored to a specific institution (Bellow, Morrisey, and Acomb 1987). Borrowing another institution's plan is not advised. A given strategic plan may be excellent for one institution or program but ineffective for another.

A strategic plan has two main purposes: (1) to specify long-term goals, and (2) to identify budget priorities. The strategic plan must be linked to a specific and flexible short-term operational plan. A good strategic plan for international recruitment will clearly identify the program's unique niches and draw a map of how to successfully enroll appropriate students into the program.

The starting point for institutions with few or no international students is different than for those institutions with some or many. However, all need up-to-date strategic and operational plans, given that recruitment of international students occurs in a volatile and complex global market.

At institutions that are just beginning to recruit international students, it is important to develop all the elements of a strategic plan, and to have both a two- and a five-year strategy. The short-term strategy is required because of the volatility of the global environment and the need for flexibility in implementation. At institutions that have been recruiting international students for many years and wish to increase international enrollment, current efforts should be evaluated and attention paid to elements that have not been addressed adequately.

Political Realities

The finest strategic plan will fail if attention is not paid to your institution's political environment. It is crucial to have the support of upper-level administrators, who are usually in the best position to make decisions that will contribute to a positive outcome. The plan will be more successful if the wider campus community is engaged at an early stage, so that all parties involved in recruiting agree on the basic premises for recruiting and recognize the potential impact such efforts will have on the academic and social environments. This will ensure that the goals and objectives support, and perhaps even influence, larger strategic plans of the institution, and that budgetary support will be forthcoming when needed. Regardless of where the impetus to recruit international students comes from, responsibility for recruitment should fall with the admission or international office.

Analysis and Assessment of Internal and External Factors

It is crucial to have solid data- and information bases. Planning depends on the availability of appropriate information and an astute analysis of the key factors that influence student choices. The internal environment must be surveyed for strengths and weaknesses; the external environment for opportunities and threats. An internal strength might be an increase in applications; a weakness, high dependence on state support. Externally, new international programs may be an opportunity; growing competition among state schools a threat (Rowley, Lujan, and Dolence 1997).

Internal Assessment. Institutions must determine how and why students decide to study in the United States and what will lead them to choose your school or program. Begin with an internal assessment of the international students who have already chosen your program or a program similar to yours located in the same region.

- Gather information about your current international students and the international experience of your faculty.

- Develop and distribute a student questionnaire to assess the admission process, sources of information about your programs, and how and why various choices were made.

- Analyze demographic factors, including the level and fields of study, gender, financial support, country and region of origin, ESL needs, and so on.

- Compare this to data on international students studying in the United States and in your particular region of the country (*Open Doors* is a good source).

- Compare with similar data on your competitors.

- Examine and analyze the ethnic makeup of your campus and community.

External Assessment. To assess the external environment you must take into account global mobility trends. Consider social, economic, cultural, and political patterns, and evaluate how your program fits into those patterns. Will your program be attractive to urban students in emerging economies who face a lack of local higher education opportunities? to the increasing number of multinational families in capital cities around the world who prefer a U.S. education? to those who need short-term training in the allied health fields?

Become current with political and economic events worldwide, and study educational changes in other countries. Sources of information include:

- International faculty

- Scholars and students

- Immigrant and international media

- Credential evaluation services newsletters (see chapter 2.3, Building Foreign Credential Evaluation Expertise for a list)

- Colleagues in international education

- Embassies and international associations

- Magazines that focus on economic trends (*The Economist, Far Eastern Economic Review*)

- Magazines that focus on educational trends (*The Chronicle of Higher Education*)

- State international trade offices

Understand the value and attraction of U.S. higher education compared with that of other countries that educate international students (e.g., United Kingdom, Japan, Canada, Australia, France, India). Also compare U.S. higher education with the educational systems in the students' countries of origin.

- Recognize and evaluate historical links. For example, consider the attraction of British education for members of Commonwealth countries, or religious affiliations linking Catholic institutions.

- Realistically assess the value and attraction of your program within this global and international context. Do your master of business administration (MBA) tuition rates compare favorably with those of Australia, for example?

- Realistically examine your competition within the United States. This is important because, given the large number of academic institutions and programs in this country, many institutions position themselves primarily locally or regionally. It is not unusual to find institutions competing regionally for domestic students and nationally (or internationally) for international students.

- Be clear-headed when learning from and assessing your competition, their offerings, their pricing, their success, and their share of international student enrollments.

A complete and effective assessment should yield a plan that clearly articulates your institution's strengths and weaknesses. The plan also will identify the most promising regions of the world and segments of international students who might consider applying to your institution. You will also have information to develop more realistically a mission and goals.

Development of Mission and Goals

It is always useful to define your mission, both to establish clarity of purpose and to provide a point of reference for recruitment decisions. A mission statement might include statements about revenue and numbers, enriching the diversity of the institution, or deepening the intellectual and cultural life of the campus. It is important that the institution be honest about its mission relative to the recruitment of international students. The market plan of an institution that wishes primarily to diversify its population will be significantly different from that of an institution that wishes primarily to increase revenue. Of course, the recruitment mission and goals must harmonize with the institution's overall mission.

The goals will identify the future direction of the recruitment effort based on whom the institution wants to recruit and what it wants its student population to look like in the future. For example, a predominantly undergraduate institution seeking to increase revenue could set as a goal the building of recognition and market in a region with few higher education opportunities coupled with a strong economic picture and a history of friendship with the United States. An intensive English program might target an emerging economy with growing foreign investment and an increased need for professionals who speak English. Goals in international student enrollment may be defined in terms of prosperity, favorable competitive position, institutional renown in certain fields or at certain levels of study, increasing enrollment or diversity, maintaining historical ties, developing new programs, or expanding the traditional campus mission.

Identification of Key Performance Indicators

Within the performance-based model of strategic planning, identifying key performance indicators plays a central role in strategic planning. A key performance indicator is a measure of an essential outcome of a particular organizational activity. It measures the outcomes of the various steps in the strategic planning process, and constantly checks performance against expectation. This performance measure ensures that the strategic plan remains practical. The plan itself should be specific, simple, and quantifiable. For example, a key performance indicator may be that 10 percent of the incoming class is international, or that the recruitment yield is the same as or higher than that of domestic students. The plan's success is judged by whether the specified outcome is realized. The selected indicators form a basic foundation for the trategic plan and ensure that the values, goals, action plan, and objectives are operational, measurable, and, above all, practical (Rowley, Lujan, and Dolence 1997; Dolence, Rowley, and Lujan 1997).

Identification of Objectives and Action Plan

Objectives that are identified within a strategic plan are considerably different from those in an operational plan. An operational plan, which is not covered in his chapter, spells out how you are going to implement your strategic plan and might include specifics on staffing; budget recommendations; admission criteria; program acceptance; target countries; use of faculty, alumni, and students; and overseas contacts. Strategic objectives are less precise than operational ones and focus more on positioning than on specific accomplishments. They frequently identify where the planner wants to be at some point in the future—in international recruitment, the recommended imeline must be less than five years—and then work back to the present to plot he path to the goal. Marketing goals and target audiences must be prioritized. So, an undergraduate institution may decide to increase international enrollment in its allied health programs by 20 percent in five years, or a graduate program may decide to ensure that their engineering programs will be well known in the Middle East in three years. There should be a multiyear and a short-term plan, given the volatility of the international student market and global political and economic trends. Allow ample room for flexibility and creativity. Be realistic about your objectives. Make sure each one is feasible, measurable, and fits your strategic analysis, mission, and goals. Compare these to the key performance indicators identified earlier.

Accountability helps ensure that an action plan will be implemented. Plans are most effective if they are set on an annual basis. For example, you may decide to strengthen recruitment in one region and expand to two new regions each succeeding year. Timelines are developed, strategies are created, on- and off-campus infrastructure is outlined, and staff and resources are identified. An annual review must be built-in to adjust strategies and review progress. That review will be more likely to remain up-to-date with swiftly changing global and regional trends if it includes information from sources used earlier in the external environmental scan, including colleagues in the same field of work. International education practitioners generally are collegial and generous with information and help.

Identification of Resources, Needs, and Expenditures

The systematic identification of needs and resources is often overlooked when planning an international recruitment strategy. Conduct an audit of resources currently used and resources that will be needed to support the strategic plan. Outline resource projections including technology for each part of the plan. This is also a time for research and advocacy. If you are able to show that the investment will meet and even exceed mission and revenue goals, your institution will be more likely to assign resources to this plan. Documented progress on key performance indicators will support future budgetary allocations for recruitment activities. Comparative information on the staffing and budgets of similar programs is also useful.

BUDGETS SHOULD INCLUDE ALLOCATIONS FOR:
• Staffing
• Postage and mailings
• Telephone, fax, and e-mail
• Web site
• Advertising
• Publications
• Travel
• Memberships and newsletters
• Reference library

Assessing Success

A sound strategic plan produces successful enrollment and retention of international students. The danger is that the plan may become outdated quickly. Periodic evaluations of the recruiting plan and its impact on the campus environment can help an institution make mid-course corrections, such as adjusting outdated assumptions about the recruiting pool or reallocating resources from one service area to another based on student usage and demand. In an increasingly temperamental market, the plan has to be malleable and responsive. The administration must be informed and updated about international student flows, so that the admission staff may be given the autonomy to make necessary adjustments to the plan.

Finally, make sure that everyone who contributed to the process is acknowledged and receives a summary of the plan. Contributors should receive an executive summary annually. Solicit and incorporate feedback. Building ongoing support for the international recruitment effort is crucial to the success of the strategic plan. Student enrollments will quickly show you how effective your strategic plan is. Figures 2.2-1 and 2.2-2 on page 40 offer two sample plans.

Reference List

Bellow, Patrick J., George L. Morrisey, and Betty L. Acomb. 1987. *The Executive Guide to Strategic Planning.* San Francisco: Jossey-Bass.

Dolence, Michael G., Daniel James Rowley, and Herman D. Lujan. 1997. *Working Toward Strategic Change: A Step by Step Guide to the Planning Process.* San Francisco: Jossey-Bass.

wley, Daniel James, Herman D. Lujan, and Michael G. Dolence. 1997. *Strategic Change in Colleges and Universities: Planning to Survive and Prosper.* San Francisco: Jossey-Bass.

hl, Norman P. 1983. "Institutional Research and Strategic Planning." In *Using Research for Strategic Planning,* ed. Norman P. Uhl. San Francisco: Jossey-Bass.

FIGURE 2.2-1
SAMPLE PLAN I

SECTION A: MISSION AND SITUATIONAL ANALYSIS

- Mission analysis
- Situational analysis
- Review of internal/institutional data
- Review of external/environmental data
- Compilation of strengths, weaknesses, opportunities, and threats

SECTION B: MARKETING GOALS AND AUDIENCES

- Prioritized marketing goals
- Prioritized target audiences

SECTION C: STRATEGIES

- Marketing action plans (including follow-up)
- Budgets
- Timelines
- Evaluation mechanisms

Source: Robert A. Sevier, "Those Important Things: What Every College President Needs to Know About Marketing and Student Recruiting." *College and University: The Journal of the American Association of Collegiate Registrars and Admissions Officers* 71, 4 (Spring 1996): 9-16.

FIGURE 2.2-2
SAMPLE PLAN II

1. Select the initial planning committee.
2. Introduce the process.
3. Establish appropriate key performance indicators and organize key performance areas.
4. Survey the environment.
   - Assess external opportunities and threats.
   - Assess internal strengths and weaknesses.
   - Perform cross-impact analysis.
5. Share results with larger audience.
6. Develop definition and measurement criteria.
7. Measure current performance.
8. Establish two- and five-year goals.
9. Determine strategies in each area.
10. Establish broad-based support.
    - Develop appropriate polices for each key area.
    - Begin implementation process.
    - Measure performance frequently.
    - Perform one-year substantive review and modification.

Source: Rowley, Lujan, and Dolence, 1997.

Building Foreign Credential Evaluation Expertise

BEFORE AN INTERNATIONAL RECRUITMENT PLAN is put in place, an institution must develop and maintain expertise in the evaluation of international credentials. An institution must be able to assess applicants' academic backgrounds and predict their potential for success at the institution. Someone at the institution must become proficient at analyzing foreign records. In the absence of the necessary expertise, students may be placed improperly or awarded too much or too little advanced standing or transfer credit.

Ideally those responsible for international recruitment should be proficient in assessing the academic records of applicants. Individuals who can combine the roles of recruiter and evaluator can speak knowledgeably about the educational background of the applicant and articulate the academic preparation and background needed to be successful at the institution.

From the international student's perspective, the array of academic programs and social and academic environments at more than 3,500 accredited U.S. colleges and universities is confusing. In addition to the wide range of curricula and degree programs, factors such as size, location, academic offerings, cost, and local environment are key elements prospective students consider as they choose a college. These factors lead students to apply to U.S. institutions based on reputation or the experiences of people they know. Evaluators must understand the system and the environment from which each student comes, and match their knowledge of the foreign educational system to the needs of the student.

An equally important piece in the college selection puzzle is the role international admission officers play in predicting the success of applicants. Evaluators initially approach the task much as they would for a U.S. applicant. The cornerstone of each evaluation is past academic performance with secondary input provided by standardized test scores, recommendations, class rank, leadership positions, and activities (or in the case of graduate students, research goals). The approach is the same; however, the differences encountered when comparing educational systems soon become obvious. Those differences constitute the challenge in interpreting foreign credentials. For example, the Scholastic Aptitude Test (SAT), a timed, objective, multiple-choice test, may have less credence as an evaluative tool for international applicants than for U.S. students. Class rank and academic letters of recommendations, common in the United States, are less so elsewhere and may not be available at all.

The Imperative of Credentials Expertise

International evaluators must possess a keen understanding of their own institution, accompanied by an ability to assess applicants from a variety of

---

NACES

The National Association of Credential Evaluation Services, Inc. (NACES) is a nonprofit membership association of private organizations that evaluate educational credentials from other countries. Incorporated in Delaware in March 1987, NACES sets basic standards for private foreign educational credential evaluation services in areas such as library resources, the experience and expertise of senior staff members, and customer service.

From 1967 to July 1970, the U.S. Office of Education (USOE, now the U.S. Department of Education) evaluated foreign educational credentials on request. This free service, offered for more than a century, was used by universities and colleges, secondary schools, agencies of the federal and state governments, private organizations, professional associations, and employers who needed to make an education-related decision concerning an applicant or client. Individuals also submitted their own foreign educational credentials to determine their eligibility for various types of further education, professional licensure, or employment.

The Comparative Education Staff of USOE provided this evaluation service, conducted research on foreign educational systems, and published that research for the benefit of the U.S. academic community. In 1966, the research and publishing activities were discontinued. In 1969, the credential evaluation service was curtailed. In July 1970 it was terminated.

To fill the gap, private foreign educational credential evaluation services were established in the years after 1970. There are now more than 50 such private services in the United States. They serve foreign-educated applicants referred to them by persons who have to make an education-related decision and who do not have sufficient knowledge of other educational systems, institutions, and programs. No licensing or accreditation process exists in the United States for foreign educational credential evaluation services. Anyone can engage in this activity, formally or informally.

In the mid 1980s, with encouragement from USOE, a team of representatives from nine evaluation services developed articles of incorporation, bylaws, and membership standards for an association. These documents were submitted to a panel of experts in this field, drawn from the leadership of the American Association of Collegiate Registrars and Admissions Officers (AACRAO) and NAFSA.

The panel reviewed the NACES organizational materials, made some revisions, and then applied the standards for membership to each of the nine participating services. The foreign educational backgrounds using an applicant "profile" for each country comparable to that established for U.S. applicants. The latter ability is described in the report of the 1996 Milwaukee Symposium, "Refining the Methodology for Comparing U.S. and Foreign Educational Credentials" and it is available on the NAFSA web site at http://www.nafsa.org/educator/milsymp/intro.html. According to the authors, "Admissions officers must be able to compare different types of academic preparation, find commonalities and deficiencies and present these comparisons logically and in ways that address the academic realities of departments and programs." The report includes a format for "institutional self-analysis" and a worksheet that an international credential

panel concluded that eight of the nine met the NACES standards for membership, and those eight became the charter members.

To become a member of NACES, a private foreign educational credential evaluation service must meet the following requirements:

- It must be private and independent. It cannot be a branch, division, or subsidiary of any other organization.

- The senior evaluation staff members (that is, those responsible for credential evaluation policy and for determining equivalents to U.S. educational credentials) must have had a minimum of five years of full-time experience (or the part-time equivalent) as a foreign educational credential evaluator at a regionally accredited university or college in the United States or at a NACES member organization.

- The senior evaluation staff members must have shared their research results with other persons in this field through conference presentations, professional workshops, or publications, so that the quality of their work could be judged by their peers.

- The senior evaluation staff members must demonstrate their knowledge of foreign educational systems by preparing evaluation reports based upon sets of educational credentials given to them by the NACES membership committee.

- The organization must submit to the NACES membership committee for review information concerning its organizational structure; its owners, officers, and directors; its reference library; and various aspects of its service to customers, including application materials, fees, and procedures for handling follow-up requests and complaints.

Since its incorporation in 1987, NACES has expanded from 8 to 14 members. Collectively, they serve approximately 100,000 foreign-educated applicants each year.

NACES member organizations contribute to the field of international education by making professional presentations and conducting workshops at state, regional, and national conferences attended by foreign student admission officers and foreign educational credential evaluators, by conducting special training programs, and by publishing information on foreign educational systems. ■

Jim Frey

evaluator can use to "review, quantify, and qualify" the institution's undergraduate admission policies for use as benchmarks in determining what is to be expected of international applicants.

To a novice credential evaluator, this role may initially appear daunting, but if it is approached in a systematic manner anxiety will soon dissipate as knowledge and expertise are developed. Over time, as the institution accumulates results with the enrollment of students from certain countries, the academic performance of those students becomes the yardstick against which future applicants from the same educational systems can be measured. Although this approach is very valuable, evaluators need to be aware of certain variables that demand that they not over-generalize. Prime among these are English-language proficiency and personal adjustment skills.

An understanding of the factors that determine academic success within various educational systems complements foreign credential analysis. Early in the evaluation process, differences become readily apparent. This is illustrated by comparing grades awarded in countries with British-based education systems with grades awarded in the U.S. system. In the British system, grades of "D" and "E" are acceptable passing marks; "C" is considered better than average. In the United States, a child who receives a "C" is average; "D" is below average," and "F" marks failure.

Expertise in international credential evaluation is acquired through training, experience, or a combination of the two. A first step in building such expertise is membership in two associations whose missions focus on international education and admission. NAFSA and the American Association of Collegiate Registrars and Admissions Officers (AACRAO) provide professional literature and training opportunities for international credential evaluators at all levels. Colleges and universities benefit directly from international evaluation expertise developed at both organizations' conferences and workshops, because a trained credential evaluator is more likely to make judicious admission decisions.

NAFSA and AACRAO both offer full- and half-day workshops preceding their national conferences as well as numerous sessions in their conference programs. Sessions for evaluators range from "Freshmen Admissions," for beginners to "Fraudulent International Credentials and Document Verification" or "Methodology for Comparing Foreign and U.S. Educational Credentials" for veteran evaluators. Other conference workshops and sessions on credentials from specific countries or regions of the world provide updates on educational systems. These are useful to foreign credential evaluators at all levels of experience. In this field, even the most experienced evaluators work to expand and update their knowledge base and discuss "impossible" cases with experienced colleagues.

In addition to formal training, conference attendance provides a credential evaluator with an informal opportunity to meet and interact with colleagues from other institutions who can serve as valuable sources of information.

Handouts from workshops and sessions become valuable resources and information mainstays in the international admission office.

Some colleges and universities contract with private, nonprofit evaluation services rather than build the expertise on their own campus. Many such services exist. Some focus on evaluation of education from a particular part of the world; most offer broad support services for credential evaluation. Some publish references on foreign educational systems and offer training workshops, translation services, and consulting. Information about upcoming workshops is routinely mailed to NAFSA and AACRAO members and may be advertised in professional newsletters. There are more than 40 agencies across the United States that evaluate credentials. Some belong to an association called the National Association of Credential Evaluation Services (NACES). Membership in NACES has entrance requirements, including screening for credential evaluation knowledge.

A week-long Summer Institute for College Admissions Professionals and Secondary School Counselors, offered by the College Board, features an international admission track that covers a range of topics. Following the institute, AACRAO offers an optional two-day workshop on foreign credential evaluation that provides instruction on general methodology and information on specific credentials from key foreign educational systems.

NAFSA's "Principles for the Admission of Foreign Students" (1981) address the role and training of personnel who evaluate foreign educational records. The association's "Statement of Professional Competencies for International Educators" (1995) cites specific qualifications for professionals with admission responsibilities. Both of these documents are available on NAFSA's web site.

Developing a Resource Library

The most important tool for foreign credential evaluation is an adequate resource library of publications about the educational systems of the world. Each institution should develop its own library for use by admission professionals and should include general references as well as country- and region-specific materials. NAFSA's "International Admissions Bibliography," scheduled to be updated in 1999, provides a list of resources that focus on the evaluation, admission, and placement of students with foreign educational backgrounds at U.S. institutions.

Some of the most useful and current resources may not be found on bookshelves in a credential evaluator's office but on the Internet. Of particular interest is a joint project of NAFSA's Admission Section (ADSEC) and its Overseas Advisers Group (OSEAS). The two groups have collaborated to create a web site that organizes content relevant to the higher education systems of the world and provides direction to other resources, such as the United Nations Educational, Scientific and Cultural Organization (UNESCO), the European Union, national ministries of education, and national education resource centers. The site may be found among the admission resources on the NAFSA web site.

At first glance the International Admissions Bibliography and other resource directories may appear overwhelming and confusing, especially to beginners. That confusion lifts with the realization that some publications are more essential than others if you are starting from scratch. The bibliography provides a framework on which to build and later add or update materials useful to the institution. Resources needed on campus depend on the numbers of students evaluated, the diversity of education systems represented in the applicant pool, and the programs and degrees offered by the U.S. institution.

SELECTED SOURCES OF INFORMATION

NAFSA Publications
tel: 202-737-3699
http://www.nafsa.org
A Guide to Educational Systems Around the World
International Admissions Bibliography (available on the NAFSA web site)
Milwaukee Symposium Report (available on the NAFSA web site)

AACRAO Distribution Center
P.O. Box 231
Annapolis Junction, MD 20701
tel: 301.490.7651 (catalog available)
fax: 301.206.9789
http:// www.aacrao.com
PIER World Education Series
PIER Workshop Reports
PIER Special Reports
Country Guide Series
International Academic Credentials Handbook, Volumes I–III
Academic Credentials Handbook
The Guide: A Resource for International Admissions Professionals
Foreign Educational Credentials Required for Consideration of Admission to Universities and Colleges in the United States

International Education Services of the College Board
1233 20th St., NW, Suite 600
Washington, DC 20036-2304
tel: 202.822.5900
fax: 202.822.5234
e-mail: Internatl@collegeboard.org
Directory of Overseas Educational Advising Centers

Materials that provide overview information about educational systems provide a good foundation on which to build a resource library.

AACRAO's *International Academic Credentials Handbook* summarizes benchmark credentials from selected countries and offers reproductions of sample credentials. Worksheets from experienced credential evaluators provide an overview for each record and a recommendation as to where the "veteran" evaluator would place a student within the U.S. educational system.

The Guide: A Resource for International Admissions Professionals includes information on the evaluation of foreign credentials, placement of international students, English-language proficiency tests, and immigration regulations.

Foreign Educational Credentials Required for Consideration of Admission to Universities and Colleges in the United States (fourth edition) offers information

Educational Credential Evaluators, Inc. (ECE)
P.O. Box 514070
Milwaukee, WI 53202-3470
tel: 414.289.3400
fax: 414.289.3411
http://www.ece.org
ECE Presents Publication Series

International Education Research Foundation, Inc. (IERF)
P.O. Box 66940
Los Angeles, CA 90066
tel: 310.390.6276
fax: 310.397.7686
e-mail: info@ierf.org
http://www.ierf.org
The Country Index

World Education Services (WES)
P.O. Box 745
Old Chelsea Station
New York, NY 10013-0745
tel: 212.966.6311
fax: 212.966.6395
http://www.wes.org
World Education News and Reviews Newsletter ■

on more than 200 educational systems and includes names of credentials along with the appropriate placement level for a student holding such a credential.

A Guide to Educational Systems Around the World, a revision of NAFSA's 1990 title, *Handbook on the Placement of Foreign Graduate Students,* covers secondary as well as higher education. The guide profiles more than 156 countries, detailing names of certificates and diplomas, the length of programs, and grading scales.

Country- or region-specific resources are essential for in-depth evaluation of specific systems and credentials. References include:

Projects in International Education Research (PIER), a joint committee of NAFSA and AACRAO, with representation from the College Board, publishes several kinds of reports about foreign educational systems. "PIER Workshop Reports" are written by multiple authors and may be about multiple countries in a region or one very complex country. Together they provide information on the educational systems of more than 80 countries. Volumes in the "World Education Series" are written by one or two authors about a single country and provide an in-depth description of the country's educational system. Both types of publications contain descriptions of educational systems, grading scales, fields of study, degree and credentials awarded, sample documents, and placement recommendations approved by the National Council on the Evaluation of Foreign Education Credentials. "PIER Special Reports" are similar to Workshop Reports in content covered but do not include placement recommendations. "The Country Guide Series" published by AACRAO provides data on the educational systems of 33 countries from Afghanistan to Zambia.

The Country Index provides charts of educational systems; identifies key certificate, diploma, and degree programs; and provides a guide for decision making that reflects the opinion of the author.

Even with a resource library in place and regular attendance at training programs, an international credential evaluator will encounter problematic or unknown credentials, documents, and institutions because educational systems change without notice. Even experienced evaluators often frequently face the unknown. Fortunately, assistance is available through networks of people willing to be contacted for assistance.

- NAFSA's ADSEC maintains an evaluators' network list that provides the names of volunteer credential evaluation veterans with expertise in a specific country's educational system.

- Educational advisers in the overseas advising centers in the credential's country of origin can be contacted for information and clarification. The College Board's Office of International Education annually produces a Directory of Overseas Advising Centers that includes advisers' names, mailing addresses, fax numbers, and e-mail addresses for more than 365 advising centers worldwide. (Appendix D lists various organizations that support American style international schools overseas.)

The INTER-L listserv is managed by a group of volunteer international educators and is hosted at Virginia Polytechnic Institute and State University. Information on how to subscribe is available on NAFSA's web site (click on Links from the home page, then on Listservs). INTER-L offers the opportunity to exchange information with colleagues, but the list managers do not verify the accuracy of that information. A feature of INTER-L allows users to specify the type of information they wish to receive; thus, an admission officer may specify that he or she wishes to receive admission-related information, but not information on immigration regulations or English as a second language (ESL) programs.

- The Internet is revolutionizing access to information for credential evaluators. Many organizations, institutions, and educational systems have their own web sites or are linked to other sites. An amazing array of information can be obtained through skillful use of web search engines. When valuable material is discovered, bookmark it for future reference and share your bookmarks with colleagues.

International credential evaluators play a significant role in the success of their institution's international program. They are the people who maximize the opportunity for international students to become contributing members of the campus community in their individual quest for academic success. By accomplishing this feat, credential evaluators ensure that the institution meets its ethical responsibility when it recruits and enrolls students from overseas. To do this effectively, they have to be at the top of their professional game, and it is only with the highest level of institutional support that credential evaluators get there.

Reference List

Schatzman, Margit A. "Methodology for Credential Evaluation: A Tool for Evaluating Foreign Education." In *A Guide to Educational Systems Around the World*. 1999. (Washington, D.C., NAFSA).

International Academic Credentials Handbook, Volume 1. 1988. (Washington, D.C., AACRAO).

International Academic Credentials Handbook, Volume 2. 1989. (Washington, D.C., AACRAO).

International Academic Credentials Handbook, Volume 3. 1992. (Washington, D.C., AACRAO).

The Guide: A Resource for International Admissions Professionals. 1994. (Washington, D.C., AACRAO).

Enrolling International Students and Exchange Visitors — Issuing Forms I-20 and IAP-66

ALTHOUGH MANY DIFFERENT CLASSIFICATIONS of nonimmigrants may study at U.S. educational institutions, the vast majority of international students hold either F-1 (academic), J-1 (exchange), or M-1 (vocational) visas. Institutional approval must be granted by INS in the case of F-1 and M-1 students, or the Department of State (DOS) in the case of J-1 students. The regulations governing the approval process are detailed and can prove daunting. Moreover, the two regulatory agencies hold different philosophies about nonimmigrants, thereby complicating the picture. DOS sees the J-1 exchange visitor visa as an important foreign policy instrument; INS views F-1 and M-1 students as two of many classes of aliens to be managed. Thus while the paperwork required by each regulatory agency is similar, the actual approval process is very different.

Approval of Institutions to Enroll Nonimmigrant Foreign Students: F-1 and M-1 Visas

As with so many aspects of INS regulations pertaining to foreign students, those governing the approval of schools to admit F-1 and M-1 students can be rather confusing. Failure to complete the INS application procedures properly can result in inordinate delay and even denial. In addition to the following summary of the application process, readers should consult the INS regulations at 8 CFR 214.3, the Petition for School Approval (INS Form I-17) and accompanying instructions, and the INS 1994 policy memorandum on revised school approval policy and procedures.

Established in 1965, the current INS school-approval process seeks to ensure that schools that enroll nonimmigrant foreign students are bona fide ducational institutions capable of meeting the needs of foreign students. Today n estimated 28,000 locations (single-site schools as well as multicampus nstitutions) have been approved by INS. Once a school is approved by INS, t may issue the official document [INS Form I-20] to a prospective onimmigrant student who uses it to apply for a U.S. visa or, if already in the Jnited States in another immigration classification, to change to student status vithout leaving the country. This delegation of authority is unique in that all ther long-term visitors (e.g., employees and entertainers) must have individual etitions for nonimmigrant status filed on their behalf by their employer and djudicated by the INS before being eligible to apply for a visa or change status.

Six basic types of institutions may be approved to enroll F-1 academic tudents: (1) colleges and universities that award recognized associate, achelor's, master's, doctor's, or professional degrees; (2) religious seminaries; 3) music and dramatic arts conservatories; (4) academic high schools; (5) lementary schools; and (6) institutions other than colleges or universities that rovide "language training, instruction in the liberal arts or fine arts, nstruction in the professions, or instruction or training in more than one of hese disciplines." Three basic types of institutions may be approved to enroll M-1 vocational students: (1) two-year colleges that award recognized degrees; 2) vocational high schools; and (3) schools that provide "vocational or onacademic training." It is also possible for a school that offers appropriate rograms to apply for both F-1 and M-1 designation. (8 CFR 214.3 (a)(2))

Assuming a school falls into one of the above categories, it may proceed with the application process: completing Form I-17 and gathering the dditional evidence required. Form I-17 is a straightforward information ollection tool: name of institution and address. There are two main pieces of upporting documentation. The first is recognition as an educational nstitution. Generally, this will take the form of certification or licensure by an ppropriate public official, or accreditation by the appropriate private agency as detailed at 8 CFR 214.3(b). The regulations are very specific as to which types of chools must have which type of recognition. Failure to submit the required vidence of recognition will result in denial of the application. For example, a charter may not be submitted in lieu of a license, certification, or accreditation.

The second requirement is evidence of appropriate resources and assets. This may take the form of a description of the educational programs offered; a vritten statement detailing the size of the physical plant; the facilities for study ind training; qualifications and salaries of the teaching staff; attendance and grading policies; amount and nature of supervisory and consulting services available to students; and current finances. Recognizing the limits of its educational expertise, the INS does not provide any details about the quality or quantity of resources expected. Rather, this requirement seeks to weed out those nala fide schools established simply to collect tuition from unwitting rospective students or provide a relatively easy means for otherwise inadmissible nonimmigrants to enter the United States. In addition to evidence of appropriate resources, certain nonaccredited institutions must submit additional evidence of the qualifications of past graduates. The requirements for such evidence are found at 8 CFR 214.3(c) and are extremely specific depending

---

SOME KEY TERMS DEFINED

Immigration regulations contain terms that have precise technical meanings. Clear communication about these matters is only possible when we agree on the meanings of those terms. It is necessary to start with accurate definitions of the terms and then use them precisely at all times. Discussions often cross cultures and must transcend language differences.

Basic Definitions

- *Alien:* The term *alien* is a term of art used in immigration law. It refers to a person who is neither a citizen nor a national of the United States. It carries no pejorative connotations in this context. Similarly the use of the word "foreign," as opposed to "international," carries no negative connotations.

- *Designated school official, responsible officer,* and *alternate responsible officer:* These terms are used by the Immigration and Naturalization Service (INS) and the DOS to refer to persons who administer the F and J programs, respectively. The international student adviser is usually that person.

- *Immigration status or classification:* These terms are used interchangeably to describe an alien's legal status in the United States and his or her presumed principal purpose for being in this country.

Documents

- *Visa:* The U.S. visa is the stamp placed by a U.S. consular officer on a page of an alien's passport. The term *visa* is frequently used incorrectly to mean legal status and permission to remain in the United States. In fact, it has a more narrow and limited meaning. It indicates that a consular officer (an employee of the U.S. Department of State) has determined that the holder is qualified to apply for admission to the United States in a particular immigration classification. A valid visa does not ensure an alien's admission into the United States; the decision on actual admission is made at the port of entry by an INS official, and that officer may require certain other information and evidence as to the intentions and good faith of the applicant. Some visas are valid for several days, some for indefinite periods; but the expiration of the visa does not necessarily have any relationship to the length of time an alien may remain in the United States. The authorized period of admission is recorded on Form I-94 by an INS inspector during the admissions inspection at the port of entry.

- The basic document used by foreign students who wish to enter the U.S. in F-1 status is an *I-20AB*. A variation of this form, the *I-20MN,* is used by students in technical and vocational programs who wish to enter the U.S. in M-1 status. The I-20 is issued by the accepting school once the student has been judged to be

the nature of the institution.

Although the regulations are quite detailed and may, at first glance, appear erly complex, most academic and many vocational institutions are able to eet the requirements by submitting evidence of accreditation and

academically, linguistically, and financially admissible. It is a complex document; foreign students use it to secure a visa and enter the United States in order to attend school. The form contains a variety of crucial information including the student's financial arrangements and the school's estimate of the time for completion of the degree or program of study. Pages 3 and 4 of the multipage I-20 are often referred to as an *I-20 ID*. The I-20 ID is a record of an F-1 or M-1 student's stay in the United States. It is the document which, when properly endorsed by the Designated School Official, will be used by the student to reenter the United States. It is the basic immigration identifying document for F-1 and M-1 students only.

The I-94 *(Departure Record)* is a 3.5" × 4.25" white card that identifies the status of a nonimmigrant who enters the United States. The I-94 carries a record of the alien's entry, the alien's immigration status, and the date to which the alien is authorized to remain in this country. The I-94 is surrendered upon the alien's departure from the United States and is retained in INS files. The notation on the I-94s of F-1 and J-1 students may puzzle faculty members and administrators. Rather than entering a specific expiration date on the form, the INS official at the port of entry may enter the notation "D/S." This stands for "Duration of Status," and it means that the student can stay in the United States for as long as it takes to complete his or her program of study within the timeframe listed on the I-20AB or IAP-66.

The *I-20 ID* and the *I-94* are often erroneously referred to as the visa. They are more important identifying documents than the visa, for they show the alien's current status in the United States, while the visa only shows that the alien was permitted to apply for entry into this country in a particular immigration classification.

Form IAP-66 is issued to foreign students and scholars coming to the United States as part of an exchange program. These people enter the United States in J-1 status and are subject to a different set of regulations from F-1 students.

The *Green Card* is more properly called the Alien Registration Receipt Card, permanent resident card, or Form I-151 or I-551. It identifies the alien as a permanent resident of the United States. The "green card" was originally green in color, for several years it was blue, and the current version (Form I-551) is pink. The term "green card" has stuck. It is a laminated card, 2.125" × 3.5" in size. It carries a photograph of the alien, the date of the alien's admission to the United States as a permanent resident, and the alien registration number (an eight-digit number preceded by the letter A). Persons who possess a green card are legal, permanent residents of the United States. Generally they have all the rights and privileges of U.S. citizens except that they cannot vote, hold some offices, or hold some federal government jobs. ■

a course catalog; others (such as proprietary institutions) have difficulty gathering the required paperwork. Again, careful attention to the specific requirements listed in the regulations and detailed on the instructions to Form I-17 and the 1994 memorandum should facilitate the process.

In addition to the evidentiary requirements, the school must indicate on a separate sheet (Form I-17A) the employee(s) who will be responsible for signing the Forms I-20 and administering the reporting and record-keeping requirements found at 8 CFR 214.3(g). Each school (or campus for multicampus institutions) may have only five such "designated school officials" (DSOs) at any one time. (Elementary or secondary school systems, however, ar limited to a total of five DSOs.) The I-17A must include the name(s), title(s), and sample signature(s) of the prospective DSO(s), and each prospective DSO must certify that he or she has read and intends to comply with all the INS regulations pertaining to nonimmigrant students.

Once the application is submitted to the local office, INS will review it for completeness and make sure that the appropriate fee is attached. (Public elementary and secondary institutions are exempt from the fee requirement.) I a piece of evidence or the fee is missing, INS may return the application. A returned application may be amended and resubmitted. If more than one piece of evidence is missing, INS may deny the application. A denied application cannot be resubmitted and must be appealed to a central authority. (8 CFR 214.3(f)) Such appeals are usually even more protracted than the original application process.

In adjudicating the application, INS first examines the evidence submitted to determine whether the school is a bona fide educational institution. Again, the INS is looking to catch those "schools" established to perpetuate financial, immigration, or other types of fraud. Second, INS reviews the I-17 to determir whether the school is in fact "engaged in instruction" as required at 8 CFR 214.3(e)(iv); a school that has not yet enrolled any students is not eligible for INS approval. Third, the I-17 must indicate that the school offers sufficient classes so that an F-1 or M-1 student may meet the requirement to be enrolled in a full course of study as defined by the regulations at 8 CFR 214.2(f) and (m). Finally, INS may (but usually does not) interview a school representative and conduct a site visit.

Upon approval, the INS issues each school a unique code consisting of the three letters INS uses to identify the district in which the school is located, the regulatory identifier 214f or 214m, a four-digit number, and a three-digit suffix for any subunits or separate campuses of that school. For example, a university in San Diego with three campuses might have the codes SND 214f.0123.001, .002, and .003. The school code must appear on all Forms I-20 issued by the institution. Once a school is approved, there is no limit on the number of Forms I-20 it may issue as long as they are issued in accordance with the regulations (to students who have been admitted under the institution's tandard procedures at 8 CFR 214.3(k))

Although the regulations provide for periodic review of a school's approval and withdrawal of approval for cause after due notification and opportunity or rebuttal), INS rarely reexamines an approved institution. Evidence of a ·attern of abuse will, however, subject a school to INS scrutiny and may ıltimately result in withdrawal of the approval. For more information on school eview and grounds for withdrawal of approval, see 8 CFR 214. 3(h) and 214.4.

Designation of Institutions to Participate in the Exchange Visitor Program

:ducational institutions (or other entities) intending to operate an exchange 'isitor program must submit a proposal to the Exchange Visitor Program ·ervices Office of the Department of State's Bureau of Educational and Cultural Affairs, hereinafter referred to as the DOS. (The United States Information Agency was responsible for the Exchange Visitor Program until October 1, 1999, vhen it was merged into the Department of State.) The application for "desig-ıation" is submitted on Form IAP-37 to the Exchange Visitor Program Services)ffice in the DOS. Forms and information are available from the Program)esignation Branch of DOS, 301 4th Street, S.W., Washington, DC 20547.)rganizations whose exchange programs are "designated" by DOS become ¡nown as "exchange visitor program sponsors." The word "sponsor" is used in a pecial way in the regulations. See the section on U.S. citizenship for more nformation.

The Exchange Visitor Program originated as part of the U.S. Information ınd Educational Exchange Act of 1948 (Smith-Mundt Act) and was modified ınd expanded by the Mutual Educational and Cultural Exchange Act of 1961 Fulbright-Hays Act). The legislation mandated reciprocal exchange of people ınd ideas to promote mutual understanding between the people of the United ;tates and other countries of the world. The 1961 act defined educational and ·ultural exchange as an integral component of U.S. foreign policy.

Exchange visitor proposals take many forms. Some applicants seek to bring n exchange visitors for English-language training, some for collaborative esearch, some for the cultural exchange inherent in an *au pair* arrangement.)OS is looking for coherent, cohesive, and financially sound proposals that are ·onsistent with the broad foreign-policy objectives of the Exchange Visitor 'rogram. Before a program is designated by DOS, the organizers must lemonstrate that they have an appropriate educational or training plan and the neans and know-how to carry out the program.

In 1995 there were more than 1,200 designated J programs in the United ;tates. Approximately 180,000 exchange visitors participated in activities ranging from high-school classes to rocket science. Many organizations and institutions seek the perspectives and diversity that international visitors provide. Obtaining these valuable complements to campus life involves some investment in time and personnel, however. Prospective exchange visitor programs should allow plenty of lead time for the application process. The planning preceding the application may require additional months, as goals are set and support structures are put into place.

The application for designation can be viewed as a discussion between the group proposing the program and the experienced administrators at DOS. While the Program Designation Branch is not a source of legal advice, they do know what elements make for a successful program, and they are bound to make their designation determination based on the regulations found at 22 CFR 62. Applicants should begin preparing their application by reading the pertinent regulations carefully and then applying them to the program they have in mind. Pay particular attention to 22 CFR 62.5 and 62.9.

Advance planning is essential. Applicants should allow several months to a year for the designation procedures.

The application must include the following:

- A clear and complete description of the proposed program

- Evidence that the program will comply with Exchange Visitor Program regulations

- Evidence of the applicant's legal status

- Evidence of financial responsibility

- Accreditation or licensure, as appropriate

- Evidence of U.S. citizenship of the sponsor

- Evidence of U.S. citizenship or lawful permanent resident status of the "responsible officer" (RO) and the "alternate responsible officers" (AROs)

- A certification signed by the applicant organization's chief executive officer stating that the RO will have sufficient staff and resources to fulfill his or her obligations. (22 CFR 62.5)

The application for designation must be signed by the chief executive officer of the applicant organization. DOS is looking for an aggregate of proof that the institution is financially sound and is operating in good faith in seeking to operate an exchange visitor program.

A brief examination of each requirement may be useful.

A Clear and Complete Description of the Proposed Program. This can take the form of a concise narrative description that includes at least the following:

- Planned program activities

Selection of participants

Financial arrangements

Plans for administration of the program

Plans for staff to administer the program

Plans for training, placement, orientation, and follow-up of program staff, host families (where applicable), and exchange visitors

Plans for evaluation and feedback, continuity, and coherence

The description need not be elaborate, but it must contain evidence that the proposal is carefully conceived, well planned, and feasible. Successful programs

---

NAFSA IMMIGRATION INFORMATION RESOURCES, 2000

NAFSA publishes a variety of materials aimed at helping international education professionals deal effectively with INS regulations governing foreign students and scholars studying in the United States. The most popular and extensive of these materials is the *Adviser's Manual of Federal Regulations Affecting Foreign Students and Scholars,* available in printed and electronic form.

- *Adviser's Manual of Federal Regulations Affecting Foreign Students and Scholars, 1998 Edition,* with updates issued April 1999. Catheryn Cotten, editor, the adviser's standard reference work on immigration law and procedure affecting foreign students and scholars. The comprehensively revised 2000 edition of the manual is expected to be issued in the summer of 2000.

- *J Regulations for Beginners.* Marjory Gooding. 1998. The NAFSA *Adviser's Manual* provides the background, but the real beginner information (how to fill out the IAP-66? how to phrase a letter to a consular officer asking that dependents be issued J-2 visas?) is presented in this hands-on guide to J procedures.

- *F-1 Regulations for Beginners.* Masume Assaf and Linda Gentile. 1998. A quick reference for many F-1 procedures, this guide provides step-by-step information on how to complete forms and which forms are needed for the various applications.

- *Immigration Classifications and Legal Employment of Foreign Nationals in the United States.* Gail Rawson. 1999. This updated version of a popular 1995 title includes information on provisions affecting honoraria for B visa holders. This poster-size chart describes each immigrant and nonimmigrant classification, provides explicit information on employment eligibility and study options for visa holders in that category, and explains the documentation required in each case to obtain employment authorization.

These publications may be ordered from NAFSA. Contact information appears in the sidebar on page 46.

do not need to have a huge amount of funding behind them, but applicants must demonstrate that the program will be self-sustaining and in accordance with the legislative and regulatory intent of the Exchange Visitor Program.

The application must also indicate that the proposed program structure is adequate to the task. For example, if the proposal seeks designation for high school exchanges with homestays, the selection and training of homestay families must be well established before DOS will consider placing 15-year-old students with the program.

DOS takes a long-term view of exchange visitor programs. If a school district seeks a single instance of exchange, for example to bring in a native speaker to teach language for one semester, it might be more appropriate for the school district to bring the teacher in as an H-1B temporary worker rather than filing an application for an exchange visitor program. On the other hand, if the exchange is to be sustained over several years, the elaborate J-1 application procedure may be worthwhile.

Evidence that the Program Will Comply with Exchange Visitor Program Regulations. It takes a serious commitment of staff time to run an exchange visitor program. Although programs vary and it is possible to operate one using volunteers, the organization must understand the scope and complexity of the regulations governing the Exchange Visitor Program. Again, the best place to start in deciding if your organization wants a program like this is to examine the regulations. The language is not difficult, but the commitment required by the regulations is significant. Will your organization be able to comply with the requirements for record-keeping, insurance, pre-arrival information, orientation, housing, and monitoring? The Exchange Visitor Program is not designed for a one-year program.

Pay particular attention to 22 CFR 62.8, which outlines the general program requirements. Can your organization comply? Will you be bringing in more than five participants annually? Will your participants be staying for the required amount of time in their particular categories? (Look at the categories—each has specific regulations and duration. Do any of the categories match your needs and intentions?) Can you make a good faith attempt at reciprocity? Exchange means real exchange—not body-for-body, but some form of exchange. Will there be possibilities for cross-cultural activities for your exchange visitors? How will you make those activities accessible to them?

Evidence of the Applicant's Legal Status. Some institutions that offer designated exchange visitor programs are created by the state in which they exist. They may take the form of a school district, a college or university, a training institute, or a state-run museum. They may be formally constituted as nonprofit entities or as products of the state constitution, or in some other way that is appropriate for that state or commonwealth. Other institutions may be independently organized (a ballet company, a private art school, a private boarding school) and constituted as nonprofit entities. Others may be run by

rganizations that serve the community in other ways, such as the YMCA or the
irl Scouts. Other institutions may be privately held companies that seek an
xchange visitor program for purposes of international exchange that
implement their corporate goals while serving the overall ideals of exchange.
Vhatever the circumstances, DOS wants to see proof of the legal status of
pplicant organizations.

Evidence of Financial Organization and Responsibility. Every program
onsor in the Exchange Visitor Program has some sort of financial structure
nd organization. DOS wants to see that this organization is regularized and
istained. A good place to begin to look for this kind of documentation is with
ie person who keeps the books for your organization. A college or university
as a chief financial officer who can write a letter about the financial standing
f the institution. A camp can submit copies of its year-end financial statement.
 partnership can submit copies of its corporate tax returns, if such documents
ill help DOS determine that the partnership is financially solid and organized
 a way that will provide continuity and coherence in its fiscal dealings. It
ould make sense for an organization that seeks to place au pairs to
emonstrate that it has plans for sustained support of the exchange visitor even
 the face of a failed placement.

Accreditation or Licensure, if Appropriate. Most educational institutions
re accredited by an overarching educational organization in their region.
roprietary language schools are accredited by accrediting bodies recognized by
ie U.S. Department of Education. Camps meet requirements of their
rofessional organizations. Some training programs must comply with licensure
quirements to operate in the United States. DOS seeks proof of such licensure
r accreditation before it will designate an exchange visitor program for any
rganization. In some rare cases, accreditation or licensure may not be
ppropriate for a given institution. USIA will negotiate this kind of
quirement.

*U.S. Citizenship of the Sponsor, the "Responsible Officer" (RO), and the
Alternate Responsible Officers" (AROs).* This puzzling requirement was the
ause of much discussion when the former USIA promulgated new regulations
 1993. The requirement was meant to ensure that the entities that secure
xchange visitor programs be U.S. entities, with a portion of their governing
oards being U.S. citizens or permanent residents. In addition, the administra-
rs of each exchange visitor program operated by the entity must be U.S. citi-
ens or U.S. permanent residents. USIA took the position that, because the
xchange Visitor Program serves diplomatic goals, the representatives should be
J.S. citizens or permanent residents. Notarized certification of citizenship or
ermanent residency by the responsible parties is accepted as proof. The certifi-
ate must use the language found in appendix A of the regulations at 22 CFR
2.

Certification Signed by the Chief Executive Officer of the Applicant

***Institution Stating that the Responsible Officer Will Have Sufficient Staff and
Resources to Fulfill His or Her Obligations (22 CFR 62.5).*** This part of the
application process should be one of the first items an institution contemplate
in applying for designation. The required certification might be a complex
matter for a college or university whose chief executive officer is cautious about
overextending the institution. The duties of the RO and AROs might be quite
complex, necessitating the addition of staff if the program becomes large or
complicated. On the other hand, the duties of the RO might be relatively simple
if the organization is contemplating a small number of exchange visitors who
fall into categories readily served by existing structures.

Forming a Consortium

Small institutions sometimes seek to band together in a consortium to apply for
designation of a common exchange visitor program. Sometimes the individual
institutions cannot support the requirement that there be more than five
participants per year, but, when grouped with other institutions, they easily
fulfill the requirement. Sometimes individual institutions do not want to
commit to running an exchange visitor program on their own because they
realize that it takes considerable training and expertise to do so. Some ally
themselves with a larger institution to help get their structures in place before
applying for a program on their own. Sometimes individual institutions band
together with other like institutions as a matter of economy. DOS entertains
applications for consortia exchange visitor programs. The application process
remains the same, but documentation from each participating institution must
accompany the application. Experience indicates that the lead time for planning
activities, communicating between institutions, and training is considerable.
Count on a year's worth of planning before the application goes in to DOS.

Recruitment Techniques

Armchair Recruitment

THE TERM "ARMCHAIR RECRUITMENT" applies to any activity you can do to attract students without leaving your campus. A well-designed and assiduously executed armchair recruitment plan should be an integral part of any institution's enrollment management plan and the foundation for travel-based recruitment activities. Most of the nearly 3,000 U.S. postsecondary institutions that enroll international students do not send representatives overseas to meet students (indeed, most do not recruit); instead, they reach prospects using the means described in this chapter.

An effective armchair recruitment program requires careful planning, hard work, and communication—on and off campus, domestically, and internationally. Although armchair recruitment may be less expensive than international travel, it does require an investment of time and money.

To lay a good foundation for your plan, be sure you have staff adequately trained to manage inquiries and applications. The entire campus community—students, faculty, staff, administrators, and alumni—should be involved in, or at least aware of your armchair recruitment efforts. (See section 4, Resources and Recruitment Networks, for a detailed discussion of the use of on- and off-campus networks in armchair recruitment activities, and chapter 2.1, Preparing to Recruit, for more campus-wide preparations.)

Armchair Recruitment Activities

Few institutions will be able to employ all of the activities described below. If you are just beginning, develop an incremental plan and add activities as budget and time permit.

Establish a system to track inquiries, applications, admission decisions, enrollment, and retention. Good records will help you decide which activities work best for your institution.

Mailing Materials

Mail your catalog and application materials to the overseas entities listed below. Include a cover letter that highlights your institution's strengths.

- U.S. Information Service (USIS) centers

- Fulbright commissions

- Binational centers

- Institute of International Education (IIE) offices

- America-Mideast Educational & Training Services (AMIDEAST) offices

- Other overseas advising centers

- Department of Defense schools

- Other schools overseas, including "international schools"

These overseas resources are discussed in more detail in chapter 4.3, Resource Networks Overseas: Educational Advisers and Guidance Counselors. Addresses of organizations that support American-style and international schools overseas are provided in appendix D.

Keep your basic brochure up-to-date by printing regular inserts listing your most recent costs and calendars. You can keep large quantities of a generic four-color brochures on hand and supplement them with two-color inserts updated

---

INTERNATIONAL SECONDARY STUDENTS OVERSEAS

When evaluating statistics for the purpose of developing an international recruitment strategy don't forget that the factors that affect university enrollments also influence enrollments in secondary schools abroad. Students who attend international secondary schools tend to be mobile when it comes to their choices of higher education. The European Council of International Schools (ECIS) surveys its member schools every year. In 1997, 66 percent of the students who left school left their host country for higher education. Half of that group (a third of all students who left school) went to North America, making it the most popular destination for higher education. A 1995 survey of the international schools assisted by the U.S. State Department revealed that of the students who left school and were looking to the United States for their higher education, 77 percent were U.S. nationals, and 38 percent were host- or third-country nationals.

International schools typically have a diverse student body. To take an extreme case, the Foundation of the International School of Geneva hosts students of over 100 nationalities. Some schools may have a large concentration of third-country nationals. For example, 34 percent of the secondary students of the International School of Düsseldorf are Japanese nationals.

quarterly. Print the brochures in different languages if appropriate and if budget allows. (See chapter 3.2, Creating Effective Publicity Materials.)

Colorful posters are in high demand at overseas advising offices and secondary schools. They do not have to be updated as often as brochures. If you send posters overseas, you may find that your campus has become a familiar sight to thousands of potential students. Overseas advising centers are often not able to handle or effectively maintain supplies of small brochures. If it will not stand up on a bookshelf or will not look good posted on a bulletin board, don't send it overseas. If you don't have an international recruitment video, consider developing one. Be sensitive to cultural differences when developing

In some countries children of well-to-do parents traditionally complete at least part of their secondary schooling at a boarding school outside the home country. Political, economic, and cultural factors affect the choice of country as well as the prevalence of the practice itself. Boarding school students who consider the United States for higher education are generally found in countries that use English as the language of instruction (e.g., United States, United Kingdom, Canada, and Australia). Day students who are in the United States as exchange students in an American high school and students living in the United States with friends or relatives in order to graduate from a U.S. high school fit in the same category, as do students who attend summer programs at independent secondary schools or colleges in the United States.

Statistical information and further contacts can be made through national associations of independent schools in the United States, the United Kingdom, and Australia. International schools associations such as ECIS can also be helpful. Most of these organizations have well-developed web sites that can be useful in the initial research phases. See appendix D for a list of organizations that support overseas American-style and international schools. ■

Elisabeth O'Connell

such a tool. The narrator should speak clearly and slowly and avoid idiomatic expressions. It will be necessary to provide your video in various world television standards (NTSC; PAL N, M, and S; SECAM; and Monochrome 625/50). (See chapter 3.2, Creating Effective Publicity Materials.)

International remail and mail-consolidation services such as Global Mail Ltd., DHL, Johnson and Hayward, and TNT Skypak can reduce overseas mailing costs (and occasionally, time). Check with staff at institutions that have used such services. Ask whether they are satisfied with the service.

When mailing application materials and catalogs, don't overlook these sources within the United States that enroll or sponsor foreign students:

- Local high schools

- Private preparatory schools

- English as a second language (ESL) programs

- Embassies in Washington, DC

- Foreign consulates located throughout the United States

- Sponsoring agencies such as the African-American Institute (AAI), AMIDEAST, and the Institute of International Education (IIE)

- U.S. Agency for International Development (USAID)

- U.S. Department of Agriculture (USDA)

- U.S. Information Agency (USIA)

Advertising

Advertising disseminates your image and selective messages. You will want to combine print and electronic media to pinpoint the markets you have identified as particularly suitable for your institution. (See chapter 2.2, Creating a Strategic Plan.)

Some international publications are distributed worldwide; many are segmented regionally and often translated. Advertising in regional publications allows your program to focus on specific areas of the world where student needs match your institution's profile. Schools in the Southeast, or Roman Catholic universities, for example, would find natural markets in Central and South America; programs in the western United States may lean toward Asian markets. Conversely, you can advertise in areas where your student population is underrepresented in order to diversify.

Advertise in overseas advising magazines such as *Study in the USA; Study America* (an IIE Fair publication); *Foreign Student's Guide to American Schools,*

Colleges and Universities, (Peterson's); *ALC Press* (in Japan); *Al-Muftah* (in Saudi Arabia); or other such magazines that have proliferated throughout the world. Advertising can be expensive, so check with other institutional advertisers to see what kind of yield they have received and how satisfied they have been with their participation in a particular publication. When selecting a vehicle for your advertising dollars, consider also if the publication is intended as a reference for overseas advising offices or if it is printed in large quantities so that students can take home free copies.

Before you buy advertising space, ask about the publication's track record. Find out if the publisher screens participants for standards, quality, and accreditation. Do they monitor their distributors, excluding possibly unreliable and unscrupulous agents? Try to verify circulation claims.

What to Say; How to Say It

Wherever you advertise, be sure your message is focused. Comprehensive messages cannot be transmitted through advertising because of limited display space. Advertising is intended to disseminate image rather than substance, so be sure you know what image you wish to project. Stress your comparative advantage, the feature that makes your program appealing to international students. Focus first on the strengths of your academic programs: "Your art career begins here!" You might emphasize location: "Study in Sunny Southern California" or cost: "Quality Affordable Education. . ." Other features to flaunt are: "A Clean, Safe, Friendly Campus." Make your point with professional-quality photos as well as snappy headlines. List majors that are popular with international students. If possible, include a map that shows where your city is located in the United States, not just your state or region. (See chapter 3.2, Creating Effective Publicity Materials.)

Ask your students why they chose your program. Include items of importance to them, such as "quality of the academic programs," "airport pickup," and "help in finding housing." Have them evaluate your advertising ideas in focus groups before you make a final decision.

Avoid guarantees such as transfer admission to a particular university and, for intensive-English programs, higher Test of English as a Foreign Language (TOEFL) scores. If students will need English-language instruction upon arrival, don't promise them immediate admission to the undergraduate program.

The World Wide Web

The World Wide Web is the ideal armchair recruiting tool. It's relatively inexpensive, easily updated, practically unlimited in length, colorful, and interactive. Moreover, it disregards time zones and geographic barriers.

Add foreign student information and application materials to your web site. If students are able to download your application off the web, it saves not only printing and postage costs, but more importantly it eliminates a round trip via two postal services. Be sure to capture information on those who browse your web site. Ask them to give information about themselves (name, complete international address, e-mail address, area of academic interest, and prospective semester of enrollment) as these may turn into enrollments at some point.

Hot links from your web site to local and area attractions will provide the student with an "electronic viewbook" of your area. Include links to the academic departments, Chamber of Commerce, lodging, restaurants, tourist attractions, galleries, events, media, retail shopping, and services. Some sites include a live video camera feed to show off local scenery and attractions.

Designing an effective site is only half the battle: publicizing it is equally vital. List your site in directories and establish links with relevant national and international sites. Through the year, monitor and update the listings monthly to be sure they are current.

Commercial Web Sites

Commercial web sites are widely advertised, provide a wealth of useful information, and are often popular. In addition to being guides to various programs, they usually contain specialized and interactive features. If joining a commercial web site service, take advantage of professional design and maintenance. These sites are updated regularly with the newest look in graphics, and their webmasters are constantly trying to improve their visibility.

Whether you develop your own site, join a commercial service, or do both, develop a standard e-mail response. As with print media, devise a policy to screen unwelcome inquiries. Respond quickly to e-mail inquiries. Students used to the immediacy of the web often judge the institution by how it communicates electronically. Answer students' questions and do not ignore those not covered by a form letter or standard response. When mailing follow-up materials in response to the e-mail inquiry, be sure to send something that is different from what is listed on your web site.

continued on page 72

MARKETING INTERNATIONAL EDUCATION PROGRAMS ON THE WEB

Now that your international education program or department has its own web site, how will you announce it to the world? You've probably already registered your site with the major search engines and web directories, such as Yahoo!, Infoseek, Lycos, Excite, HotBot, and WebCrawler. If you haven't, don't wait, because it can take a long time to get into these lists.

If you're using your program's web site to recruit international students for undergraduate, graduate, and ESL study, be sure that your site is welcoming to prospective students. International students pose unique challenges to web site developers because of their language and cultural variations, the wide range of their computer and browser capabilities, and their level of access to the technology itself. On the other hand, when compared with other forms of international student recruitment, such as print advertising, student fairs, educational tours, and third-party recruiters, the World Wide Web offers an effective and affordable means to market one's international education program.

To increase your program's visibility on the web, link your web site to other sites. Some links are purchased for a fee, but many web sites allow you to promote your program at no cost. The best of these free sites provide a direct link. The next best provide only a brief description of your program with contact information. Those sites that allow you to advertise for a fee usually offer a variety of promotional services, including banner advertisement, web page construction, translation, and featured listings. The paid option can range from a couple of hundred dollars per year to thousands of dollars per month.

Best Places to Promote Your Web Site for Free

All of the services listed below are free.

- ALC Press at www.alc.co.jp publishes the popular study-abroad guides for the Japanese student market. They have created an ESL program database where ESL programs can input their program data. Specific information about this service is available at www.alc.co.jp/esl/up.

- Add your English language school's link to the ESL Cafe's Web Guide (www.eslcafe.com/search/index.html) at Dave's ESL Cafe (www.eslcafe.com).

- The Digital Education Network at www.edunet.com offers EduFind (www.edufind.com), a comprehensive search engine that includes categories for ESL schools, opportunities for international education, and other areas of interest. You must complete the Education Providers Registration Form at www.edunet.com/register.html to be listed in this directory.

- GlobalStudy's "English Programs Around the World" at www.globalstudy.com/esl is the "yellow pages" directory of ESL program web sites in the United States, Canada, Australia, New Zealand, Great Britain, and Ireland. Get your free listing in this directory by completing the Submit a Website Form at www.globalstudy.com/esl/submit. Also, ESL programs that are members of organizations whose purpose is the advancement of professional standards and

continued on page 70

quality instruction in ESL programs can receive one month of free banner advertisement on the GlobalStudy web site. This is GlobalStudy's way of promoting high standards for ESL programs around the world.

- Gradschools.com at www.gradschools.com is a popular site for international students searching for graduate programs. Administrators can add or update information about their graduate program at www.gradschools.com/update.

- Studyabroad.com at www.studyabroad.com has a directory of academic and intensive language programs. International education programs can submit free listings for inclusion in this online database using a Free Listing Form at www.studyabroad.com/update.

- StudyWorld at www.studyworld.co.kr is a Korean site that allows you to enter or update information about your ESL school using an online form at www.studyworld.net/office.htm.

- WorldWide Classroom at www.worldwide.edu offers university-based ESL programs the opportunity to complete an online University Profile at www.worldwide.edu/universityprofile for listing in a study-abroad database.

- Yahoo! at www.yahoo.com and Infoseek at www.infoseek.com are the best of the generic search engines to get a link to your international education program web site. Yahoo takes the longest to get a listing, but it's worth all the trouble and time it takes to submit your site to its popular directory.

Best Places to Promote Your Web Site for a Fee

All of the services listed below have fee-based promotional services (i.e., banner advertisement, featured listings, web site hosting, or a combination thereof). Any that offer "free" web listings require you to purchase one of their services.

- Education International (EI) Worldwide at www.eiworldwide.com provides a key-word searchable mini-profile of all their member institutions (which also have full-profile listings in one of the EI Worldwide guidebooks). As a member, you can receive a mini-profile of your ESL, engineering, business, or management programs in their online directory with a direct link to your program or university home page. Membership and ordering information is available on the EI Worldwide web site.

- International Education Service at www.ies-ed.com offers an online listing for colleges, universities, and ESL programs that participate in their student placement services and international education guides.

- Study in the USA at www.studyusa.com offers a variety of target-language education guides for international students that include information about choosing U.S. colleges, universities, and intensive-English programs. Those schools and programs that advertise in one of their guides can also receive a featured listing on their web site, for an additional cost.

Advice for Promoting Your Web Site

- Build your web site and its content to appeal to the prospective international student. Avoid the flash of cute animated banners, sound files, and heavy graphics. Make sure your pages will download quickly and be readable by any computer using any browser. Also, avoid "hype." Your web site should be accurate, up-to-date, and understandable, even to non-English speakers with limited English proficiency.

- Don't list your site if it's not yet ready. Some of the information you will be placing into these databases will be long-lasting and errors you make now will haunt you for a long time. Also, don't use "under construction" graphics. Web sites are always under construction.

- Most of the search engines reference your site via your page titles. Make sure your page titles are appropriate to your content and meaningful, such as "Study Business in the U.S.A.," or "Learn English as a Second Language." This will ensure that your page ranks higher on most of the major search engines.

- Use META description and META keywords statements in each page. The META tags that are embedded in your page's html code are used by many of the search engines as a way to allow you to control what they say about your site, and the categories under which they place you.

- Provide full contact information on the main page of your site, including your host institution's name, address, phone number(s), fax number(s), contact name(s), and e-mail and Internet addresses.

- Get your international education programs and services highlighted on the "front door" of your institution's web site. If internationalization is a major priority at your institution, ask your university to demonstrate its commitment by placing an "international button" on its home page. This will ensure that international students find your international offerings quickly and easily.

What Else Do You Need to Know?

There is a lot more to know about web-based marketing and the rules are always changing. Auto-submission software, banner advertising, electronic newsletters, newsgroups and e-mail discussion lists, cybermalls and non-web methods of site promotion are just a few of the areas that you can explore. Probably one of the most beneficial things you can do is to visit other international education program web sites and study their site structure. Also, evaluate how they use content and design to attract prospective students. If you have the time and the willingness to learn, try building and promoting your department's web site. You will always do a better job yourself because you have the most complete knowledge about your programs and the kinds of students you want to attract. ∎

Reprinted from *International Educator,* 7, 4:53–54.

Clark Egnor

Following Up

The quality and clarity of your follow-up materials are every bit as important as your initial attention-getters. So is the timing of your replies. How often has a student chosen a particular program because "they were the first to write to me." Plan carefully the design, content, timing, and sequence of your responses to student inquiries. Do you need a brochure for each of your majors? for each graduate school?

While standard response letters can cover most frequently asked questions, students will be favorable toward your institution if you respond to their concerns individually. Even if the student does not enroll at your school, you may have gained free advertising and excellent public relations because that student will share his or her good feeling about your school with parents, counselors, friends, and neighbors. Such word-of-mouth advertising may reap dividends years later. Word-of-mouth advertising has a longer shelf-life than printed publications, and it certainly carries added credibility.

Decide what to do when your program does not meet the needs of a potential applicant and how to refer this person to other programs that provide a better fit. Ethical recruiting mandates that you consider the best interests of each student.

Train enrolled students to make follow-up calls to admitted students. Ideally the students should be from the same country as the applicants, but U.S. work-study students or volunteers can do wonders for converting admitted students to matriculated students.

Participate in professional development activities offered by NAFSA, the American Association of Collegiate Registrars and Admissions Officers (AACRAO), the Institute of International Education (IIE), and other professional and membership organizations. These will help you keep abreast of international market trends and changes in educational systems and immigration regulations. They can be an excellent source of new ideas for your recruitment program. National conferences also provide a chance to network with overseas advisers, counselors, and consular and embassy officials.

Armchair Recruitment Budget

Although armchair recruitment techniques are inexpensive compared with international travel costs, there are several items that need to be factored into an armchair recruitment budget. They include:

- Professional staff time

- Additional staffing to respond to inquiries

- Printing

- Postage

- Telephone/fax

- World Wide Web and e-mail maintenance

- Search services' mailing lists or labels

- Advertising

- Video production and distribution

- Professional association memberships

- Reference library

Having developed an armchair recruitment plan, it is far too easy to sit back and hope that your plan will be successful the first time around. Do not fall into this trap. Monitor the success of your efforts, and constantly fine-tune your plan. Just as with domestic or overseas recruitment travel, the secret to successful armchair recruitment is to stick with it. Isolating the variables that enter into the evaluation equation will separate you from less successful armchair recruiters.

Finally, even though much of armchair recruitment can indeed be accomplished sitting down, it is not a stand-alone activity. Even on the tightest budget you should travel occasionally to stay close to changing trends and to hear directly from prospective students.

Creating Effective Publicity Materials

CREATING AN EFFECTIVE FAMILY OF ADMISSION MATERIALS is an important ongoing activity. Most institutions convey information about their programs, services, and admission procedures through various media.

Developing Content

Answer some basic questions before deciding on the core content of your publicity materials:

- What do students need to know when researching and applying to universities?
- When do they need to know the information identified above?
- From what countries do your current international students come?
- What new countries are being targeted for recruitment?
- How are decisions made in the target cultures?
- Who in the search process makes the decisions?
- What resources are available to increase your knowledge of the student market?

In each publication you produce, include a healthy blend of both standard and distinguishing information (Figure 3.2-1). Standard information is that which is quantifiable: tuition and fees, institution size, average class size, and basic admission requirements. Distinguishing information is much more difficult to quantify. It is information that enables readers to distinguish your institution from another: campus culture; unique features; and characteristics such as academic programs, climate, safety, or reputation. You can identify these comparative advantages through exchanges with current students and reviews of institution-wide publications. Current students can highlight the characteristics that, for them, distinguished your institution from others and made the difference in their university selection. Publications from other

FIGURE 3.2-1
STANDARD INFORMATION VS. DISTINGUISHING INFORMATION

STANDARD INFORMATION	DISTINGUISHING INFORMATION
• tuition and fees	• academic programs
• size of institution	• institutional reputation
• average class size	• campus culture
• admission requirements	• climate
	• location
	• safety
	• class profile

departments on campus may introduce you to projects, people, activities, or a specific language that may also attract the attention of prospective students.

Many institutions use a common theme or concept to link all of their publications. Often this is a standard image or tag line that is used institution-wide. Examples include "A Practical Liberal Arts Education" or "Where Leadership Begins." Sometimes development of this unifying feature is left to the international admission office: "If You Want to Learn English, Learn It in Utah" or "Study in Beautiful Maine, U.S.A."

When developing content, never lose sight of the material's intended audience. Many people are involved in a student's college-selection process, including:

* The students themselves

* Parents

* Other family members

* Friends

* Counselors

* Advisers

International admission officers who know how decisions are made in the countries in which they recruit can more readily identify important players in the selection process and target their messages accordingly.

When drafting the copy, keep your audience in mind. Although you are targeting a comparatively literate group, you will still need to use simple, standard English. Short, direct sentences or "bullet" items are most easily understood by non-native English speakers. Avoid colloquial expressions, idioms, and contractions. You may find that you need to balance your tone based on your targeted populations and institutional profile. For example, if your institution requires a high TOEFL score and you receive a large number of inquiries from unqualified applicants, you may choose to use some of your publications as a method to screen those applicants who might not meet your minimum language proficiency requirements. Use a more challenging vocabulary and mention your high TOEFL cutoff.

While it may seem enticing to have your publications available in many different languages, the reality is that production and translation costs can be daunting. If you are targeting a particular region or country, consider translating some of your supplemental pieces into a few other languages. You may also wish to direct one of these "other language" publications to the parents of interested students, since they often have more difficulty with English. If you choose to translate your publications, use extreme caution because the meaning of some words may vary from country to country or even within the same country. Have at least two native speakers proofread the text. To identify points of possible confusion, have the foreign-language text translated back into English and compare it with your original.

Identify a particular goal or desired outcome for each publication along with a timeline that represents the entire admission process. These outcomes can include:

• Requesting additional information

• Submitting the application form for admission

• Sending the enrollment deposit

Remember that each of these actions by the targeted audience leads to follow-up contact by the admission office. Personalized correspondence, whether in the form of a letter, fax, or e-mail, is ideal. However, time constraints, computer systems, volume of inquiries, and other factors can make this difficult.

As you develop your publications, identify items that speak directly to the student or other interested party. You might refer to more detailed information included in the mailing, respond to frequently asked questions, or provide an overview of the admission process. Identify the most convenient and appropriate mode by which to share this information. If you are unable to personalize correspondence, choose an appropriate greeting such as "Dear Student" or "Dear Applicant" rather than "To Whom It May Concern." If you will be personalizing your correspondence, the greeting can present a challenge, as it is often difficult to determine the gender or surname of a person. Therefore, it is a good idea to include the student's entire name in the greeting.

Design

Perhaps your campus has a fully staffed public relations office. If so, draw these professionals into the production process. Because they have most likely created many other institutional publications, you will probably not have to spend a great deal of time explaining your content. However, make sure you work closely with them during the design process to ensure that items such as cultural considerations are addressed appropriately.

If you do not have a public relations professional at your institution, you may need to enlist the assistance of a professional designer from outside the campus community. If this is the case, don't be afraid to interview a number of companies or individuals until you identify one with whom you can have an open and constructive working relationship. It is important to learn if your new partner has done work for other educational institutions or has experience in developing marketing tools for an international audience.

Whether you work with an on- or off-campus designer, remember to involve current students, faculty, staff, and alumni. They can be good sounding boards as designs are created.

When developing full-color publications, one of the early considerations is choosing the color scheme. Much research has been conducted on the emotive responses that result from certain colors and the role that culture plays in those responses; however, it is virtually impossible to choose a color palette that satisfies everyone. That said, a good rule of thumb is to work with the designer or campus public relations professionals to identify colors that are consistent with other institutional publications and that do not incorporate an overabundance of "wild" colors. Keep your color choice simple and consistent. Carefully monitor the use of flags and other national symbols.

Choose your photographs carefully. For example, show students in a traditional classroom environment rather than sitting on the grass listening to a professor. In some cultures, it would be unheard of for students and their teachers to sit on the grass. Your photographs should present a balanced view of your campus and surrounding community. If it snows in your area, for example, do not limit your pictures to clear, sun-filled days; unless you are truly near a beach, avoid seascapes. Illustrate your climate, rural or urban location, and typical residence hall rooms honestly. In the long run, your institution and your students will be better served.

Modes of Delivery

The next challenge is to determine the best way to communicate this information. These modes include, but are not limited to:

- Print
- Personalized correspondence (mail, fax, telephone)
- Video
- CD-ROM
- Internet (e-mail and the World Wide Web)

When evaluating the merits of each mode of communication, consider their cultural appropriateness, production and distribution costs, timeliness, and any technological limitations that may affect how the information is received and processed by the intended audience.

Print

Glossy, full-color publications are expensive, but international students like them as much as their American counterparts do. When sending publications to overseas advising centers, one viewbook and a catalog will probably suffice. Remember, if it does not stand on a shelf, overseas advising centers will likely not have room for it. Additional publications that serve particular purposes include catalogs; newsletters (to prospective students, counselors, advisers, alumni, parents, etc.); and brochures about athletics, student organizations, support services, majors, and financial aid. One method for stretching your publications budget is to produce a full-color viewbook that accommodates inserts of time-sensitive information, such as costs and calendars. This will allow you to print a larger quantity of the most expensive piece and then periodically reprint the inserts as the information changes.

Electronic Media

Institutional videos allow students and families to visit your campus without leaving their homes. Does your domestic admission office have a video? Is it appropriate for use in international recruiting? Ask current students who represent various cultures to review it and offer their opinions. If the response is favorable, you may only need to have it translated into different international formats. Although many schools and advising centers have dual-system VCRs (for example, NTSC and PAL or NTSC and SECAM), most prospective students and their families will be able to play only the local format. Determine if formats other than NTSC (used in the United States) are necessary. If you need to produce a video, consult with your public relations office or designer and develop a product that complements your other publications. Keep in mind the cultural differences among the countries that you are targeting, and remind your narrator to speak clearly and slowly and to avoid idiomatic expressions.

CD-ROMs have recently been added to the list of resources that can be found in the international admission office. Although many prospective students have access to computers, not all of those computers have a CD-ROM drive, nor can all drives play the latest CDs. It can be a challenge to develop a product that is meaningful in content and attractive in presentation while taking into consideration the lowest common denominator of technology. Based on your time, available technical and financial resources, and needs, you may opt to bypass the development of a CD-ROM and focus your efforts on creating a web page that in all probability will have greater reach.

The Internet

The World Wide Web disregards time zones to reach all corners of the world. Colorful, interactive web sites are relatively inexpensive, easily updated, and practically unlimited in length. Despite these considerable advantages, some questions remain:

- Will the World Wide Web be a primary publication or a support resource?

- How much information should be available on the web site?

- Is some information better communicated via other modes?

- Should information on the web be designed to encourage students to contact the international admission office for more information?

Your first page will capture your viewer's attention-make it your best page. Use a key element—whether it be a stunning photo, graphic, or a statement about your program's best feature, at the top of your text.

Keep your web site simple. Create many short documents rather than a few long ones. Use easy-to-read buttons to navigate from page to page. Keep your graphics basic so succeeding pages will load quickly, and avoid gimmicks such as counters that slow down your site, or frames that are not supported by older browsers. Include an option for navigating the site without graphics, since some of the people who will access your site may be using text-only browsers.

Provide a clear table of contents, with many options for prospective students to select: detailed course descriptions, faculty profiles, student testimonials, cultural attractions, and clear instructions for applying online. Provide every opportunity for students to linger over your web site. The more they discover about your program, the more likely they will be to apply.

The introduction of a web site will bring with it many benefits; however, a few policy and processing challenges may also surface.

- How will staff manage e-mail inquiries?

- Will a form letter response be needed to meet the increase in inquiries?

- Will the application be available via the web? Can it be completed online or will students need to download it and return it by mail or fax?

- If the application is accepted electronically, is the admission office's computer system capable of processing the application without re-keying the information? How will the application fee be collected, or will it be waived? Is there a method for obtaining the required signature at the completion of the application?

There are no magic answers to these questions, which are being addressed on campuses around the country. As you develop your web site, contact your colleagues and learn how they are dealing with these issues. Visit other institutions' web sites to see how they are using the web. Also see chapter 3.1, Armchair Recruitment, for additional information on using the Internet to promote your international education program or office.

Advances in technology have changed our need and desire for information. With more options available to communicate with prospective students and their families, it is increasingly more difficult to discern when and how to present and collect information. By taking time to consider your audience and its needs, you will be in a better position to develop admission publications that truthfully, ethically, and thoroughly convey the necessary information to your prospective students regardless of their country of origin.

International Travel

INTERNATIONAL TRAVEL is often viewed as the be-all and end-all of international recruitment efforts—a quick and easy way to add international students to your campus population, or a journey into lands usually reserved for exotic vacations. It is neither. Although it may be one of the most effective means of international recruitment available, international travel should be undertaken only after the components of "armchair recruitment" are in place. This will ensure that the added inquiries generated from international travel will be handled in a manner that will produce the best results for the institution's international efforts. (See chapter 3.1, Armchair Recruitment.)

International travel affords an institution the opportunity to make itself known in foreign countries in a way that demonstrates an active interest in international education. At the same time, the institution gains direct knowledge about the lands, cultures, and people visited. Travelers can learn how educational systems in the target countries are organized and function and how best to address students' needs for further education. Your decision to participate in a group tour, individual travel, or a combination of the two will depend on several factors.

Group Tours

A group tour offers advantages for an institution considering its first overseas recruitment trip. Having an experienced tour provider take care of essential logistical planning for the trip is the principal advantage. Scheduling two weeks of overseas appointments can be extremely taxing. Coordinating flights, hotels, and recruitment visits requires a tremendous amount of time, effort, planning, and patience. Schedules have to be created and recreated numerous times as appointments are made and cancelled or rescheduled. Most experienced recruiters find the amount of time required to organize a trip to be beyond their resources. Those new to international recruitment are cautioned to think carefully before attempting to coordinate a tour on their own. Tour organizers typically provide an itinerary and arrange air and ground transportation, hotel accommodations, college fairs, school visits, and sometimes individual or small-group appointments.

Selecting a Tour

The variables you will want to consider when deciding on a particular recruitment tour include:

- Length of trip
- Itinerary
- Pace
- Number of participants
- Cost
- Recruitment focus (undergraduate, graduate, or professional)
- Related educational opportunities (briefings, in-country materials)
- Record of success and past participants' recommendations

Be especially careful to consider the type of group and the reputation of the particular group tour you select. The students and counselors you meet will associate your institution with the tour and the other participating institutions. An inappropriate match may work against the image your institution wishes to project. Groups may focus on undergraduate or graduate students exclusively, or on master of business administration (MBA) students. Some include high school students in the tour, and some allow participation by non-U.S. institutions. When contemplating your first trip, you are well advised to ask colleagues that you know and respect for their evaluations of different tour providers. At this time, several group tours operate in Asia, Latin America, Europe, and the Middle East, with schedules available in the fall or spring.

One common function of the tour organizer is to stage college fairs for the institutions represented on the tour. The fairs may be held in a hotel ballroom or at a local exhibition center, in which case they may be open to the general public. Fairs are often held on the campus of a local high school or university, in which case they may be restricted to the students of the school and perhaps a few other participating schools. Typically, the tour organizer will advertise the event in the media and through local educational institutions and organizations. Institutions lacking name recognition in the region benefit from sharing the event with better-known institutions. Your institution gains valuable exposure from such advertising, which often is exceedingly expensive if undertaken alone, and from access to large numbers of students, who would be much more difficult to contact if traveling alone.

Some group tours include an educational component. This may take the form of briefings with ministry of education officials of the countries visited, the educational attaché from the U.S. consulate, or the staff of organizations such as the Fulbright commissions, AMIDEAST, and IIE. Briefings, which often encompass history, current economic and political dynamics, and emerging trends, provide an excellent means to improve your understanding of a foreign educational system.

Important additional sources of learning on the group tour, ones often taken for granted, are the experienced institutional representatives with whom you travel. On the plane, in the airport, on buses, and while sharing meals you will have considerable time to discuss the subtleties of international recruitment, the "do's and don'ts," successes and failures, foreign credential evaluation, and other subjects. At its best, an overseas group recruitment tour is not only one of the most effective recruitment activities, but also a traveling seminar in international education.

Group travel has its disadvantages. Recruitment tours usually offer a fixed itinerary for all participants. Although this provides benefits of scale that lower the costs associated with transportation and lodging, it limits the degree to which the program can address the particular needs of individual schools. Your institution might be interested in the recruitment of undergraduate students only, yet the tour might include venues designed to attract graduate students. Your institution may be looking to increase enrollments in your intensive English program, but the tour may focus on the recruitment of American students living abroad or on students in American or other English-speaking schools. In these situations a considerable portion of your overseas travel time may not be directed at your primary focus. Some groups will allow members to schedule individual appointments at such times; others will insist on full group participation at all scheduled events.

In addition to the countries from which you wish to recruit students, your group recruitment tour may also visit countries in which you have little interest. A country on the tour may already be overrepresented in your student body; another country may have few students likely to choose your institution. The tour may also exclude countries you would like to visit. In either case the yield on your investment will be diminished.

Although most group tour organizers are careful to schedule their trips at the best possible time of the year to reach interested students, the timing may not be ideal for you. It may be inconvenient to be gone for the length of time required, or you may have conflicting plans. Institutions that are new to overseas recruitment may find they are not recognized by counselors or students as a new member of a group of institutions, many of which may have longstanding relationships with the counselors at the schools being visited. Be patient, but always be prepared to step forward and present your institution when the opportunity arises.

Individual Travel

One must approach individual travel with a sense of adventure. The disadvantages of group recruitment travel may lead you to undertake an individual recruitment trip, or, after absorbing many of the advantages of group travel, you may feel ready to construct an itinerary tailored to your institutional interests. However you come to the decision to travel alone, be sure you have sufficient institutional commitment, support staff, and time available to carry you through the more involved process of planning and scheduling.

The representative traveling alone will have to begin thinking very early about the countries to be visited and the events and appointments to be made. As a first-time exercise, it is advisable to start at least a full year in advance by constructing a planning calendar (see appendix E). There is a distinct advantage to establishing your own itinerary. You can select the countries you want to visit, stay as long as you want, and make appointments that are appropriate for your school. An experienced travel agent can help you find appropriate hotels at corporate or discounted rates and the most efficient airline routings. Select travel agents carefully and be sure they understand that your itinerary is likely to change several times.

One of the main advantages of traveling alone is the opportunity for individual appointments where the focus is one-on-one communication about your institution. Appointments can include off-campus visits with students, agents, alumni, and consular officials, as well as campus visits with school counselors and students. Such visits, often held in a quieter atmosphere than that found at a college fair, allow you to present the unique programs of your institution and to learn more about the students and institutions you are visiting. The experienced recruiter will select a variety of appointments to best address the institution's enrollment goals and the demands of their travel schedule.

The lobby of your hotel often serves as a comfortable, convenient, and cost-free place to meet with individual students and families. Meeting in your hotel room is generally not advisable. Meeting rooms can be booked for a dinner with alumni, or for a small gathering of prospective students.

Organizations such as the Fulbright commissions in Europe and IIE in Asia sponsor large international education fairs each fall. These offer the individual recruiter a means to contact large numbers of prospective students without being tied to a group tour. Because the timing of these fairs is coordinated within the region, they provide a convenient framework for an itinerary that will include individual visits and meetings. (See chapter 3.4, Education Fairs.)

Costs

The cost of individual travel will differ from that of group travel, not necessarily in the amount spent but in how it is spent. Money may or may not be spent on acilities for group events. Advertising or announcements in local media may be onsidered but will be much more costly than when shared by a large group. ιny advertising you purchase will, however, be specific to your institution, and nay be worth the additional costs involved. If you elect not to produce a special rochure to use on the trip, as most participants in group tours must do, the noney you save can be converted to activities such as alumni meetings; ntertaining prospective students, their parents, or parents of currently enrolled tudents; or visiting additional countries.

Mailings to institutions and students to announce your visit may entail onsiderable cost. Plan ahead, to take advantage of international remailers or ulk surface mail rates for large events. Military post office (APO and FPO) ddresses may be available for some large sponsored events; APO and FPO ddresses require domestic postage rather than international postage, but lelivery time is lengthened. Using telephone, fax, and e-mail to make and eschedule appointments with counselors, agents, prospective students, their amilies, and alumni, is costly and time consuming; you may end up paying nore for these items than if traveling with a group.

cheduling

t goes without saying that these activities need to be planned well in advance. n particular, you should be well prepared for first-time visits to schools and ιniversities. Begin by identifying "feeder" schools—schools from which your nstitution has enrolled good students in the past and others that could become ;ood sources of students. In many cases these will be American or international chools abroad. They are excellent sources of undergraduate students who have een exposed to a U.S.-patterned curriculum. Typically, the student body :omprises one-third Americans, one-third local, and one-third third-country nationals. In many countries you will also find highly qualified students at elite national schools that offer an international curriculum or a combination of an nternational and local curriculum. For details on how to contact international ιnd American schools overseas see appendix D. If you are trying to recruit ;raduate students, target local universities and the general public.

When requesting appointments at host country schools, keep in mind that he public school counselor or university faculty member's first responsibility is :o send students to local universities. They may have no interest in, or may in act be opposed to, sending their students to U.S. institutions. Part of your job vill be to explain opportunities for their students and generally promote ;oodwill on behalf of U.S. higher education. Don't write off such counselors or aculty members, but visit them consistently over the years in hopes of helping hem broaden their views of your institution and of U.S. higher education. Many are protective of their students and will screen where the students go to chool, not unlike their counterparts in the United States.

Be sure to follow up in writing to make specific arrangements for each visit planned. In the letter of confirmation, reiterate the purpose of your visit and the amount of time your schedule allows. Call upon arrival in each country and city to confirm your appointments. If changes need to be made, try to accommodate everyone even if the revised schedule isn't particularly convenient for you. As you set up appointments, get directions to schools and agencies, including maps. Leave plenty of time between visits in case you get lost or your trip takes longer than expected.

Whatever the type of visit, send as much appropriate information as possible in advance. Don't assume that the counselors, professors, or agents with whom you will be meeting know anything about U.S. higher education in general or about your institution in particular. They may not be aware that their

ADVANTAGES AND DISADVANTAGES OF GROUP AND INDIVIDUAL RECRUITMENT TRAVEL

Group Travel

Advantages
- Multiple schools raise larger crowds. You will meet more prospective students.

- You expand your network of professional colleagues. You will learn from them while traveling.

- Most group managers provide training.

- All arrangements are made for you. Although this is built-in to the trip fee, it is very efficient and cost effective for you.

- Costs of events, advertising, and transportation are shared. One school cannot afford to do for itself what a group can do together.

- Local personnel like to serve many schools with one effort.

Disadvantages
- There is no time for local personnel to meet you personally so you can explain your programs.

- No "memory" of you or your institution remains.

- Your school is often not distinguishable among the whole group of schools.

- The itinerary may include places or programs that are not appropriate for your institution.

- The timing of the tour may not fit your schedule.

previous students have attended your school. They may not know much about the U.S. university application process, or conversely, they may have graduated from a U.S. university. Assess their level of knowledge to the fullest extent possible, being sure to be culturally sensitive and to avoid making assumptions.

Bring materials to present personally and allow ample time between appointments to allow for delays or changes in format. Before ending a visit, be sure to secure in writing the names and titles of those with whom the appointment was held, along with other important officials. Send a short thank-you note, preferably before moving on to the next country, and, if feasible, any follow-up information that was requested. Put the counselor, faculty member, principal, school, agent, or alumnus on a list for future mailings. Make notes on all meetings as soon as possible. The facts of one appointment quickly blend

Individual Travel

Advantages

- You can adjust the itinerary to meet the needs of your institution.

- You can target your recruitment for a specific program to a specific audience.

- All of the appointments will be relevant to your institution.

- You have more free time to explore the environment and identify opportunities for your institution.

- When you make a personal visit, local personnel remember you and your institution.

- Local personnel take time to meet you personally so you can explain your programs and the distinguishing characteristics of your school.

- Local personnel become more informed and will tell students of your institution after you have left the country.

- The students you meet are more likely to develop an interest in your school.

Disadvantages

- Advertising in multiple countries for one school is very costly.

- It is time consuming to make all the arrangements for an individual tour on your own.

- You will see fewer students.

- It is more expensive to entertain or see groups of students.

- Individual travel can be lonely.

- You get no feedback from others; you return with only what you were able to observe. ■

with those of the next if careful notes are not taken. Once back home, write personal letters to students to encourage them to apply. Follow-up is critical to the success of the entire trip.

Who Should Be the Recruiter?

Finally, who should be the recruiter for your institution? The answer will depend on the organizational structures in place at individual institutions and the skills and experience of staff members. Sometimes the responsibility will fall to one individual and sometimes to several individuals, depending on institutional size, level of commitment to international educational exchange, and the type of students sought. Recruiters will most often be part of your admission office, international admission office, or faculty.

Many institutions improve their results by housing several international functions together in one unit. Under such an arrangement, international admission and recruitment, international student advising, and study-abroad professionals work cooperatively to create a coherently managed enrollment and services model for all international educational exchange activities at the institution.

Whatever your structure, it is incumbent upon institutions to send representatives who have enough time to plan adequately for the trip. They should have good public-relations skills, cross-cultural interest and sensitivity, and an understanding of the educational systems of the United States and the countries to be visited, as well as the academic programs of their own institution. They should also be known to follow through on their responsibilities.

Education Fairs

EDUCATION FAIRS provide personal contact with prospective students and impart lasting first impressions. Fairs often provide families with their first personal exposure to U.S. higher education. International students appreciate the opportunity to meet representatives from multiple accredited institutions in one place and at one time.

Education fairs abroad may provide the university with the most economical way to meet prospective students. All arrangements are made for the participating schools, and the representative has only to arrive to staff the booth. But remember that the fair environment does not allow a lot of time for qualifying the many leads you may develop. Smaller schools may find this recruiting environment too impersonal and rushed for the type of recruiting they wish to do.

Types of Fairs

Since the early 1980s, there has been a steady increase in the number and types of fairs worldwide. Fairs in which U.S. schools participate come in a variety of forms, ranging in size from 10 to more than 200 participating institutions. The types of fairs include:

- Education and career fairs. These tend to be the largest fairs because they may include local and international schools, as well as companies looking for employees. They are often held on more than one day and usually draw the biggest crowds because of the variety of options offered. However, the crowd will be the least focused.

- Multiple-country education fairs. These fairs include institutions from several countries, so students visiting these fairs may not be focused on U.S. education and may still be in the process of deciding in which country they will study.

- American education fairs with institutions offering various levels of education. This type of fair attracts students interested in attending an American high school, college, or university.

- American education fairs limited to higher education. This type of fair attracts students interested in attending an American college or university.

- International and American MBA fairs. These fairs are very popular and attract a more mature, professional group of visitors.

Smaller fairs are more personal and less bewildering to students. The most obvious advantage of a smaller fair is its slower pace, which allows more opportunity to talk with students to see if there is a good match. One of the disadvantages of a smaller fair is less exposure to the market, and fewer students in attendance.

Larger fairs usually draw greater numbers of students and, as a result, a larger number of possible matches with the institution. At larger fairs, well-known institutions invariably attract disproportionate groups of students at their tables, but they also draw bigger crowds to the fair in general. Larger fairs also create an opportunity for exchange of ideas with counterparts at other institutions. You can observe how other institutions present themselves and can find out what experience other representatives have had with other fairs. Some of the drawbacks of larger fairs are the impersonal atmosphere and limited time to assess individual students.

Venues vary from a basic table and chair outdoors to state-of-the-art exhibition halls that provide private booths and professional services. The standard of the venue will naturally be reflected in the registration fee.

Fairs can last from four hours to three days. Exhibitors are expected to have a representative present at their table for the duration of the fair. An empty table leaves a negative impression.

One measure of a well-planned fair is the briefing. It is important for the representatives to be well informed about local educational, social, economic, and political issues before meeting the students, their parents, and local educators. Presentations for students regarding application procedures, student visas, financial aid, and other topics may be offered in conjunction with the fair.

Selecting Fairs

Ask the fair organizer some basic questions to determine whether the fair would be a good match for your school.

- How many other colleges and universities are expected to participate? If your school is relatively well known, this should not matter. If not, a larger fair would draw more students and give your school more exposure, increasing your chances of attracting suitable applicants.

- How many students are expected?

- What other types of schools are expected? Participants may include a variety of types of institutions, such as ESL schools, American boarding schools, local branches of American colleges, and MBA programs.

- What are the most popular fields and levels of study in that country?

- What does the fair organizer provide? Some fairs offer signs, backdrops, bottled water, meals, briefings, translators, and so on. You may want to find out if the venue is air-conditioned if this is of particular concern to you.

- How, where, and how often will the fair be advertised? Is publicity included in the fee or is there a separate charge?

Ask questions of several sources to help you determine which fairs are most appropriate for your institution. Past participants from schools similar to your own can help you decide whether the fair would be a good match for your school.

- How well is the fair managed?

- Does the fair organizer try to help solve problems during the fair?

- Is the venue comfortable? Is the atmosphere conducive to meeting students and parents?

- Are the National Association for College Admission Counseling (NACAC) guidelines applied and enforced? (See appendix C.)

- What percent of visitors are serious about studying in the United States?

- Have students from the country in which the fair is located been successful in obtaining U.S. student visas?

- How much material can one expect to distribute?

- Was the fair a success for recruitment purposes? Would you attend it again?

Making the Most of an Education Fair

Do your homework. Familiarize yourself with the educational system and culture of the country you are going to visit. Understand the local academic credentials with respect to your institution's admission policies. There may be students at the fair who attend international schools with different educational systems or who have been educated in other countries. You may need to be aware of a variety of educational systems.

Talk to students from the countries you plan to visit who are currently enrolled at your institution. They may know of potential applicants interested in meeting you, have a good sense of which fields of study are popular back home, and suggest strategies to make the fair more productive.

Notify local contacts of your participation in the fair. Even though the fair organizers may contact many of the same people, your personal invitation may encourage people to attend the fair and visit your booth. Among those you might attract are alumni, parents of current students, school counselors, as well as representatives from English-language schools and private and public educational organizations. Invite school counselors who have sent students to your college to meet you at the fair.

Invite one or two alumni to assist you at the fair. Enthusiastic bilingual alumni greatly enhance your presence and are valuable during busy periods, particularly if local parents do not speak English.

What to Take

Most college representatives prefer to travel light. They send materials to each city in advance to their hotel, to an alumnus, or to the fair organizer. Try to have the following general materials on hand at each fair:

- At least one set of sample catalogs for each level of study offered by your institution for reference (most representatives do not distribute catalogs, which are bulky and expensive to ship).

- Viewbooks and photo albums to help students visualize the campus and its setting, as well as general information that describes the overall educational experience and highlights the strengths of the institution.

- Application materials and procedures for both international and American students.

- Information on entrance requirements; costs for tuition, room, and board; popular majors, and a U.S. map showing the location of your school.

- Brochures on specific popular and unique fields of study, including undergraduate, graduate, ESL, short-term programming, and distance learning. An alternative is to put copies of these in a binder for reference.

- Information on student life, campus activities, residence halls, student organizations, international student support services, and so on.

- Inquiry or response cards for students to complete at the fair so you can follow up when you return to campus.

- Your business cards so students can contact you in the future.

- Name tags for alumni.

- Souvenirs from your campus for alumni.

- A one-page information sheet translated into the local language.

- A modest university banner to identify your institution and make your table look attractive, if fair guidelines allow.

Be realistic. Seek advice from past fair participants to help you determine how much material you will need and how many of the students you meet may be serious. Also, try to get a sense of the type of students you will see in each city (e.g., undergraduate, graduate, MBA, ESL, engineering) and send or bring appropriate materials. The quantity of materials you send will depend on the student market and your institution's size, name recognition, and range of programs. Code the applications differently for each fair you attend so that you can monitor each fair's success.

Carry a supply of materials with you in case your shipped materials get lost in transit. Always have a plentiful supply of inquiry cards, business cards, and a one- or two-page information sheet that can be photocopied if necessary.

Find out from fair organizers the best way to send materials. Different countries have different customs regulations; in some cases, duty may be charged. Some fair organizers have permission from their local U.S. consulate for schools to use the APO or FPO address; however, APO and FPO shipments can take up to 10 weeks. Fair organizers will provide you with information on sending materials via air and sea.

How to Present Your School at the Fair

At a busy fair where you may not have a chance to chat with visitors individually, give a short presentation that answers basic questions, then ask for specific questions. Be prepared to respond to generic questions on life and studies in the United States, particularly at fairs that attract institutions from many different countries.

If you are not a full-time admission officer, you may want to attend a stateside college fair with someone from the admission staff before traveling overseas. Watch the way they handle crowds and answer students' questions.

If the facilities at the venue permit, bring a laptop computer on which samples of your school's web page can be shown as well as any other information you may want to make available to students in the country you are visiting. Students may be curious to know, for example, how many students from their country are enrolled currently, what they study, and the activities in which they participate.

Representatives and alumni are expected to stay behind their tables during the fair and are encouraged to distribute relevant academic information to help fair participants assess which university will be the best match for them. Professional behavior is encouraged at all times. Represent your institution well and refrain from making negative remarks about other institutions.

Students expect representatives to know the admission requirements for all of the academic programs at their institution. Representatives should be able to encourage or discourage applicants and to answer questions about application procedures.

Your alumni can play an important role at the fair; they prove that your graduates do return home and succeed. They can also serve as a link between potential students and the college after establishing contact at the fair. Alumni provide firsthand knowledge about the college from a student's point of view, which is sometimes the most credible form of information. Contact alumni far enough in advance so that they have time to identify who will help you at the fair and can spread the word of your visit to interested students. Be sure to allow time to brief the alumni before the fair on current campus issues, important admission and scholarship policies for international students, and how you would like them to respond to questions.

Students often feel overwhelmed at a fair. They may be tentative about approaching representatives. A smile and a friendly manner may be your greatest tool. Always be polite; anyone you meet at a fair is a potential student or contact. Never snub anyone, even those that appear not to be a good match for your institution.

In addition to students and parents, counselors, agents, or company representatives offering various services may approach you. It is important to verify the legitimacy of these visitors before considering a working relationship. (See chapter 4.4, Working with Third-Party Recruiters and Agents.)

NACAC NATIONAL COLLEGE FAIRS RULES

The National Association for College Admission Counseling (NACAC) has adopted rules governing college recruitment fairs. Here are the association's guidelines on booths at the fairs.

Booth Displays

NACAC makes every attempt to keep the focus of the National College Fairs on education, not promotion. Prefabricated displays may not exceed eight feet in height and must be placed in the rear of the booth. Institutions may not contract for or set up elaborate displays.

You may distribute only brochures, catalogs, and other appropriate items that provide a factual description of your institution and its programs, and you may do so only from your booth. *Plastic bags, calendars, bumper stickers, buttons, pennants, posters, candy, or any other advertising or promotional material may not be distributed from the booths.*

Demonstrations such as preparing food, drawing caricatures, cutting hair, or similar activities are not permitted.

Audiovisual equipment is permitted and must be confined to the registrant's booth. All audio equipment must be used at low volume, and noise levels kept to a minimum. NACAC reserves the right to determine at what point sound constitutes interference with others and must be discontinued.

Following Up

After the fair, it is very important to communicate with the students you met so they will continue to think about your school. Most schools have very organized follow-up programs for domestic students, but not for international students. Competition for international students is growing and continuous correspondence with potential students is essential to make your recruitment program a success.

- Schedule interviews with serious prospects, either with you immediately after the fair or with alumni at a later date. Results of the interview may be useful to the admission committee, and the interview will create a solid tie between the applicant and your school.

- Immediately contact students who stopped by your table and completed inquiry cards, thanking them for their interest in your college and providing them with specific information you may have promised to send them.

- Sustain contact with those students by sending them additional information about your school based on their interests and questions.

- If you distributed applications at the fair, what kind of follow-up will you send? Consider sending a letter from the department chair

Aisles in front of the booth must be kept completely clear of promotional and display materials. The aisles will be swept and cleaned, but registrants must keep their own spaces clean and in good order at their own expense.

Booth Staffing

Admission staff members or alumni are allowed as exhibitors at the National College Fairs. Alumni representatives are expected to have completed a thorough training program with their respective institutions, and to be able to answer knowledgeably the specific questions asked by students and parents. Copies of NACAC's *Guidelines for National College Fair Alumni Representatives* are available upon request.

Each individual who is registered to staff a booth must wear a name badge. Exhibitors are required to wear name badges to be permitted access to the booth area at the designated times before the opening of the fair.

No more than three representatives shall staff an institution's booth at any one time. ■

Source: NACAC *National College Fair Rules*. 1999. National Association for College Admission Counseling. Reprinted with permission. Contact information for NACAC appears in appendix C. NACAC's guidelines are followed at most overseas fairs by U.S. universities.

describing the unique characteristics of the university or curriculum or a letter from a current student from the prospect's home country.

- Thank people who may have helped you and keep in touch with local contacts such as alumni and people in advising centers and schools.

- Make notes while the event is fresh in your mind, listing pros and cons of the fair to help you decide whether to attend again. Make a list of materials that would have been useful. Note how you would do things differently next time. If possible, provide the fair organizer with constructive criticism on how to improve future fairs.

Are international education fairs worthwhile? It depends on your institution's needs and goals, the type of students you are hoping to enroll, and whether your institution's infrastructure can accommodate international students. There are hundreds of American university representatives who consider regular participation in overseas education fairs part of their recruitment plan. Whether they are still in the process of building name recognition for their institutions or are simply maintaining a presence overseas, they are part of a growing number who use fairs as an important recruitment tool. For current information on fairs and tours that participate in fairs, subscribe to and participate in INTER-L, a popular listserv used by members of NAFSA and others. Also check the web sites of international educational organizations, and read their newsletters.

SUBSCRIBE TO INTER-L

INTER-L, a free electronic forum, was founded by international education professionals interested in using the Internet to assist other professionals in the field. Today, the list is managed by volunteers, and policies are determined by a committee of interested international educators with experience running listservs. Although many INTER-L participants are members of NAFSA and other organizations in the field of international educational exchange, and although the products, services, and policies of such organizations are often discussed by INTER-L participants, INTER-L is not affiliated with, overseen, or supported by any organization.

To subscribe, address an e-mail message to: LISTSERV@vtvm1.cc.vt.edu. In the message area, type: SUBSCRIBE INTER-L. Leave the subject line blank. The listserv will respond with instructions on how to proceed. Once your subscription is complete, you will receive full instructions on using the listserv.

Resources and Recruitment Networks

Building an On-Campus Recruitment Team

WHEN MOST PEOPLE HEAR THE TERM "on-campus recruitment team," they think in traditional terms of admission personnel. Involving faculty, students, and staff outside the admission office in international student recruitment is not unheard of, but it is most often restricted to armchair recruitment activities (see chapter 3.1, Armchair Recruitment). Moreover, when non-admission personnel are used in direct recruitment abroad, it is usually by default rather than as part of a comprehensive strategy. In fact, a heterogeneous team can be useful in all types of recruitment.

The Benefits of Teamwork

The obvious benefit of an on-campus recruitment team is the support it gives to the efforts of the office charged with international student recruitment. By making those efforts more effective and dynamic, the team provides increased international visibility for the entire institution. A less-obvious benefit is the opportunity to strengthen the institution's academic reputation through the involvement of faculty members who are experts in their fields. The faculty can offer students insight about particular programs that complements the information provided by admission officers. For example, suppose you want to promote a program in audio engineering recently begun by your institution. Who better to talk about the curriculum than the faculty who designed it?

A team approach may help you extend your budget. Suppose that a department chair is scheduled to lecture at a conference in Hong Kong and offers to assist the admission office while there. This is a wonderful opportunity—the recruitment trip's biggest expense, travel, is already paid for by the administrator's department. The particulars of budget sharing in a situation such as this may vary somewhat from institution to institution, but in all likelihood your cost would be minimal. Having an on-campus recruitment team also affords a staffing advantage: in essence it allows you to be in two places at the same time.

As your faculty colleagues learn the nuances of international recruitment and admission, they develop an awareness and appreciation of the process. This is especially true after they have witnessed the complete process, from first meeting students in their home countries to having them set foot on campus. Once they understand the process and its challenges, they are much more likely to support your efforts by providing the necessary resources. Involving your colleagues in the process is the best way to engender a sense of ownership and appreciation.

Getting Started

Begin building an on-campus recruitment team by identifying one individual within the institution to serve as team leader. This individual will be responsible for all aspects of team development and coordination. Because so much of what the team will do revolves around international admission and recruitment, the team leader should have a strong background in both areas and be a member of the international or domestic admission team that makes admissions decisions about international applicants.

Once the leader is in place, the next step is to identify potential team members among your faculty and staff. A questionnaire or survey is the most effective way to reach potential team members. The purpose of the questionnaire is to elicit information relevant to the potential team member's ability to assist in recruiting efforts. The questionnaire should be preceded by a statement about the relation of international student recruitment to the institution's mission. Your potential team members must understand and agree to adhere to the principles of ethical recruitment before they become part of the team. (See NAFSA's Code of Ethics, appendix B.) The questionnaire itself should be clear and brief. Ask questions about international travel experience, participation in international seminars and conferences, future international travel plans, contacts abroad, current involvement with international students, and interest in helping with the recruiting process. (See the sample questionnaire in appendix F.) Include a list of recruiting activities for which candidates could offer their services. Those activities might include interviews, college fairs, receptions, school visits, and network building.

The questionnaire should be sent to anyone you believe may in some way be able to contribute to your recruiting efforts, no matter how limited the assistance. Your list might include faculty, the president, vice-presidents, trustees, and directors of various units who may travel. Consider any special relationships your college or university may have with foreign institutions, agencies, and governments and include individuals associated with those programs. Take the time to send the questionnaire directly to selected faculty and administrators, as opposed to forwarding it to deans and chairpersons only and asking them to pass it along. Indicate a date by which you would like to receive responses. Bear in mind that the process of developing your team will take some time. Therefore, send out the questionnaire well in advance so that you can schedule visits appropriately. Begin at least a year before the desired start date.

Screening and Selection

Once you have collected responses to your questionnaire, you are ready to begin the screening and selection process. Consider the skills listed below as you go about determining who would be good candidates for the on-campus recruitment team. Some are required skills for almost any position dealing with students in a college or university setting; others relate specifically to interaction with international students. The questionnaire responses will provide initial guidance in identifying candidates who possess the desired skills. Based on responses to the questionnaire, meet individually with selected candidates to better assess their appropriateness as team members.

An ideal team member has the following profile:

- Awareness and sensitivity to other cultures

- Ability to communicate and interact comfortably with the target audience (parents, counselors, and students)

- Thorough knowledge of the institution he or she represents

- Experience in international travel

- Contacts in the international arena

- Foreign-language skills (helpful but not required)

- Willingness to promote your institution

- Flexibility and patience

- Willingness to commit to the team for multiple years of service for program continuity

If there is one quality that is an absolute must, it is cultural sensitivity. You may find individuals who are experts in their fields, but if they are not culturally sensitive, they will not be effective team members. In the recruitment process, the first impression is vital in establishing a relationship between your institution and another organization or individual. You do not want a team member to jeopardize that relationship through cultural gaffes. In your selection process look for colleagues who have interacted with international students, such as advisers of international student groups. Faculty and administrators with international teaching or study-abroad experience, former

Peace Corps volunteers, and recipients of foreign grants such as Fulbright, Marshall, German Academic Exchange Service (DAAD), and Humboldt are also good candidates.

International travel experience is an advantage when selecting a potential team member, especially if the travel was work-related. However, the fact that a professor or administrator has traveled extensively overseas does not automatically qualify him or her for your team. Consider all of the other desired qualities in conjunction with the travel experience. It is also imperative to select members who are volunteering to join the team because they want to help you and the institution in the recruitment process. Their perception of their role may be very different from yours. They need to understand what is expected of them. At a minimum they should be prepared to make a one-year commitment. If they prove to be effective, ask them to remain with the team for an extended period of time.

As you go about the selection process, think about how you can match team members' skills with your particular recruitment objectives. Ask them how they can contribute to achieving those goals. Review the questionnaire to see which recruiting activities the candidates offered to perform. Some members may only be able to contribute minimally, but they should not be excluded. It is in your interest and that of the institution to be as inclusive as possible without compromising the standards set out in the selection process.

Training the On-Campus Recruitment Team

Having selected your on-campus recruitment team, you are now ready to begin training. Training the team is by far the most labor-intensive step of the entire process. It is time consuming because team members, although specialists in their own areas, may have had little or no experience with international recruitment and admission. You have to accommodate work and travel schedules, making group training for the most part impractical. To help reduce the amount of individualized training, develop a manual that includes a list of the questions most frequently asked by international students along with responses to those questions. Team members should be able to respond to those questions before they depart. If members are not comfortable discussing program offerings and general admission information, have them participate in some admission functions on campus such as information sessions, open houses, and receptions. If time permits, have them sit in on admission interviews with prospective international students.

Once general training has been completed and a schedule set for a particular trip, meet with each team member again. At this point, the training should include an overview of the following:

- Goals or objectives of the trip
- History of recruitment in the target region
- Background of target audience and contacts
- Educational systems and credentials
- Protocol and cultural sensitivity
- Materials they will be taking with them

Discuss the desired goals or objectives of the trip and the format of the events in which the team members will participate. Bear in mind that a team member who has not done this type of work previously may not know what to expect. Help team members prepare for discussions with the target audience by summarizing your institution's relations with the people they will be visiting. Walk them through the schedule appointment by appointment. Don't assume they are experts in international travel just because they have previous international travel experience. Finally, encourage them to take notes throughout the trip. These notes will prove helpful later when writing a trip report.

One of the most critical aspects of the training is an overview of the educational systems team members will encounter and the foreign credentials they may be asked about. Team members need to understand the basics to have credibility with their audience abroad. Knowledge of the educational system demonstrates a level of interest and sophistication on the part of the representative. Be sure to have someone who is well versed in foreign credential evaluation do the training. Ideally, this would be someone within the institution who can also discuss institution-specific admission requirements. Your training manual should contain a description of the target educational systems and credentials as a helpful reference during the trip.

As soon as team members return from a trip, meet with them for a debriefing while the details of the trip are still fresh. Ask them to submit a written summary or create a report format that they can fill out while traveling. Specific details include who they met, the content of the meetings, the outcomes, the commitments made, and any follow-up required. Go over all of the notes and ask them to tell you what did or did not work. This will be useful in assessing specific visits and as a reference for future trips to the target region. Be sure your office follows up with contacts made during the trip as necessary. Remember that team members have other responsibilities and reporting to you may not be their top priority, especially if they have been away from the office or classroom for some time.

Limitations

For all the benefits generated by an on-campus recruitment team, several limitations should be noted. Chief among them is the fact that most team members are volunteers, and you can demand only so much of them. In many cases, when faculty and administrators offer to assist while traveling abroad, they are combining your agenda with theirs. If they have only half a day to devote to recruiting, you have to make the most of that window of opportunity. Although it may be common practice for an admission officer to make four school visits in a day, that is not advisable for new team members, even if their schedule allows it; it may discourage them from volunteering for future trips simply because it is too taxing. For similar reasons, it is not advisable to plan trips that are longer than a couple of weeks.

A second limitation in the use of an on-campus recruitment team is the inability to monitor performance and thus to exercise quality control. You can only rely on the team member's own assessment of a trip. If team members do not perform as expected, or if they embarrass the institution while traveling, you have little recourse. In most cases you won't even find out about it unless a disgruntled student, parent, or counselor calls to complain. By that time, the damage will have been done. To help ensure this does not happen, you should contact traveling team members regularly to ask them about questions they may not have been comfortable answering. Offer advice on how to respond to difficult questions. After the trip, and for future reference, seek feedback from alumni and counseling colleagues about the team member's visit. In the end, you have to make a leap of faith.

How do you measure the effectiveness of the team's recruitment activities? The team's recruitment activities in a given year are limited and sporadic. You may have several different people recruiting in the same city in any given year. In such a situation, it would be unfair to judge success solely on the basis of a single visit even if the individual were an experienced international admission officer. Instead, you may want to consider having the same team member visit a particular city or region over a period of time. This will provide continuity in the recruitment process while allowing you to better measure the efficacy of your recruiting strategy for the target region. As with most international recruitment strategies, you need to make a three-year commitment to be able to see significant results. Establish a benchmark by looking at the numbers of inquiries, applications, acceptances, deposits, and enrolled students from the target recruitment territory. Compare each of these numbers from year to year. Ultimately, you will be able to measure success by determining if there has been an increase in the number of qualified students who enroll from the target recruitment territory.

Using Your Team in Direct Recruitment

One of the best ways to ensure that team members are adequately prepared to travel on their own is to have them travel initially with someone experienced in international recruitment. This approach has many benefits. First, it allows you to set up the schedule according to your particular needs. Second, it allows you to train the team member under controlled conditions. Third, a team with a range of skills and expertise offers more to your audience, making it easier to obtain appointments at schools, foundations, and overseas educational advising offices. Team travel also allows for the widest array of recruiting activities during a trip.

You will have screened your team to determine the activities for which each member is best suited. Regardless of their institutional role, nearly any team member can be helpful in establishing new networks or expanding existing networks of international contacts. International faculty, in particular, may have contacts who are able to help the institution in the recruiting process perhaps through former students, now alumni, who are anxious to help their alma mater. These contacts can prove to be an invaluable resource in opening doors to ministries of education, corporations, universities, high schools, and educational foundations. Faculty and administrators may have foreign-language skills and a knowledge of the educational system and culture of the target recruitment market. The background information they gather while traveling and the contacts they establish provide the resources necessary to better assess the viability of a particular market. Based on their information, you will be able to decide if follow up is warranted, what types of recruiting activities might be appropriate, whom you should visit, and where you should go.

Another recruiting activity with which team members should already be familiar through their on-campus training is the college fair. Because most international college fairs are similar to domestic fairs, they are a good introduction for new team members. As with any college fair, if you have alumni, study abroad students, or parents of current students in the area and the fair permits their participation, ask for their assistance. They will prove very helpful in answering questions and lending overall support to the team.

Student Participation

Students can contribute in many ways to the recruitment team, although their role in direct recruitment is restricted by the academic calendar. To identify potential volunteers, target young people who have been active in clubs and organizations, especially those with an international focus. International student associations and model United Nations are two excellent pools from which to draw good candidates. You might also seek recommendations for student team members from faculty and administrators, particularly if you have programs in international studies or related areas. Don't forget to include your intensive English program if you have one.

To screen and select student team members, use a questionnaire and personal interviews, just as you did with faculty and administrators. As you go about the process, bear in mind that students may not have the faculty and administrators' range of experience and skills. This fact should not detract from their candidacy, however. Cultural sensitivity and the ability to communicate and interact with others are the qualities that are most essential for this group. Look for students who have already been good ambassadors for the institution and those who would likely make good leaders.

The next phase of the process of building an on-campus recruitment team with students is training. Given the demands placed on them as full-time students, training should be limited to preparing them for specific tasks they are to perform. Students should not be expected to discuss all facets of the college or university they represent. Another team member, such as an admission officer, should accompany them whenever possible. International student team members provide their biggest contribution in direct recruitment through school visits and college fairs in their home country. While in their countries of origin, students can help by calling prospective students to share their experiences and answer questions from a student perspective. Later on in the admission process, if your institution hosts a send-off reception for newly admitted students from a particular country, be sure to involve currently enrolled students. This is an excellent opportunity for new students to bond with the institution and ensure higher enrollment in the fall.

Making the Most of Alumni Contacts

AMONG A SCHOOL'S BEST REPRESENTATIVES are its students and alumni. When your school is thousands of miles from the applicant market you want to target, the amount of information you can provide long-distance through publications, the course catalog, the Internet, and other media is limited. That is why so many schools are turning to their international alumni to bridge the gap. Personal testimony about the value of the educational experience your school offers can be a powerful marketing tool overseas.

Involving Alumni in International Recruiting

There are many reasons why colleges and universities involve alumni in their international recruiting. Here are just a few.

Enthusiasm

There is something very powerful about enthusiastic alumni. In domestic recruiting, word-of-mouth marketing from graduates has long been known as a great source of applications. Word of mouth is even more powerful with prospective international applicants. In many countries the development of relationships is a critical part of the culture, so international students and their families will pay particular attention to an enthusiastic graduate whom they know.

Experience

There is a certain camaraderie and understanding in relating one-on-one with fellow countrymen and countrywomen. Many alumni have overcome obstacles in going abroad, providing inspiration to prospective applicants and the belief that their own goals can be reached.

Networking

International alumni have an amazing network. Many have attended the same high school, are involved in the same professional organizations, and are concentrated in one or two large cities. Sometimes parents of alumni can promote your institution abroad. Do not ignore the contacts that successful, powerful parents may have in a foreign country.

Credibility

Too many prospective international applicants rely on spurious rankings and vague institutional reputations. Local credibility helps lesser-known schools. The stamp of approval from fellow countrymen and countrywomen helps reassure parents and gives them comfort in their decision to send their sons and daughters to study abroad.

Cultural Knowledge

Alumni can be an excellent source of cultural knowledge. By talking to current students and alumni you can get an inside view of their countries' economic and political situations and uncover trends that may affect your applicant pool. Alumni also know their own educational systems and the selectivity of certain universities in certain fields. They can help you target high schools and universities in their countries. They will often give you invaluable knowledge about influential families, and the potential leadership possibilities of various candidates. International alumni can be a great source of information and help with logistics for the admission officer who travels and recruits alone. American alumni living abroad can also provide information about the culture and region, not to mention their ability to translate the American educational and cultural experiences to potential applicants.

Vested Interest

International alumni have a vested interest in the reputation and future of your school. They know that improving the student body adds value to their diploma.

Budget

Not every school has the budget and personnel to travel overseas to recruit. Even those who can travel can't be everywhere at once. In the absence of a staff member from your institution, alumni can represent your institution at overseas educational fairs, visit high schools, conduct student interviews, and host receptions for prospective students.

Alumni Records

Accurate records are crucial to the success of an alumni recruitment program. Make sure records of permanent home addresses are correct at graduation and see that they are transferred to the alumni office.

Keep international alumni informed about the progress of the university. It may cost more to send mailings (newsletters, magazines, notices of regional activities) to the international alumni, but they are as interested as domestic students in the development of their alma mater. They may want to find ways to help the institution, and an alumni recruitment program is a valuable way for them to contribute.

Selecting Alumni Representatives

Choosing the right spokespersons is critical. You will need to work with the alumni office and any other necessary campus constituencies to identify the characteristics you would like your alumni representatives to possess. Work closely with the international student and alumni offices to identify active alumni around the world. Strong alumni support is likely to reflect and further stimulate a strong market for applicants.

Some admission offices choose current students to help them by giving tours, hosting information sessions, conducting on-campus interviews, and serving on the admission committee. Such students can be your international alumni admission representatives "in training." Get involved in international student activities on campus and get to know groups of international students. Send a congratulatory card before graduation and invite them to talk with you about joining the alumni network. Some schools choose as their alumni admission representatives a mix of recent graduates who are familiar with the current campus atmosphere and older alumni who have demonstrated career success.

It is important to keep abreast of alumni activity and your institution's involvement in targeted regions of the world. Consider organizing "regional update meetings" at which admission officers, career services administrators, current international students, recent alumni, and faculty with an interest in the region get together to share knowledge and discuss potential issues related to your applicant market and recruiting strategies.

Organizing

You can formally or informally organize your alumni to represent your school. Some schools use alumni in their domestic recruiting regionally; each region has its own alumni admission representatives. Others have informal alumni counselors who are listed in their catalog and on web sites. Still others have admission office liaisons within each of their alumni clubs. Your method will be determined by the organizational structure of your school or department and what works best for your situation. When those responsible for current international student programs, international alumni relations, and recruitment abroad develop a coherent strategy based on international recruiting intentions, alumni presence, and institutional resources, success can be expected. Monitoring relations among key groups with the help of the alumni office is well worth your time. Use e-mail to remain in regular contact with alumni and to monitor their success. Even though many admission offices use teleconferencing, interactive video, and web-based inquiry and application systems, you will never be able to replace the impact of an international student talking one-on-one with another.

Training

Your volunteers must be well informed in order to be effective. Train them in the following areas:

- New and current academic programs
- Accomplishments of the faculty
- The latest student-body profile
- Current admission policies and procedures
- Costs
- Financial aid and scholarship possibilities
- International student services
- English as a second language (ESL) programs

You may want to include a discussion on rankings, global and regional trends, or topical issues unique to your school. If you can't afford to meet directly with your alumni, provide an alumni recruiter's handbook, send current literature (including a course catalog), create a listserv, and use e-mail to update alumni on current campus issues.

If possible, train your future alumni representatives before they graduate. Schools that can afford to do so bring alumni admission volunteers back to their campus for a weekend of training every few years.

Activities for Alumni Admission Representatives

In your communications, maintain the distinction between alumni, who may volunteer to help the school identify and attract prospective students, and professional institutional representatives. Alumni should always be clear of what their recruitment responsibilities entail. Alumni admission representatives can become involved in many activities. The most popular include the following:

Identifying and Referring Applicants. Alumni may identify excellent candidates for your programs. Keep track of their referrals in your database. An annual report showing how alumni representatives have been helpful in the recruiting process can be invaluable.

Education Fairs and Forums. Alumni can provide important support at overseas education fairs. You may be swamped with questions that alumni can answer. Some of the students and many of the parents may not speak English well. Alumni who speak the local languages can be extremely helpful. In many foreign countries, parents are much more involved in making college choices than are students, so it is important that their questions be answered. Professional schools may want to seek out recent graduates and high-ranking alumni to help at your booth, espousing the spirit of the current campus environment while testifying to your program's potential for success. Well-trained alumni can represent your institution at fairs that you may be unable to attend.

Information Sessions and Receptions. Ask your alumni to serve as hosts for information sessions about your school. Use them as panelists at question-and-answer sessions. Have them partner with their company to sponsor the reception, giving "name power" to your school and reception. Have your alumni give an information session at meetings of their secondary school, college, or professional organization. One school allows prospective students to reserve seats for such receptions via their web site. Overseas educational advising centers and test prep centers will often welcome information sessions led by alumni. Many schools are vying for their attention; your alumni's personal touch may help these centers get to know your programs and give them a permanent local contact. (See chapter 4.3, Resource Networks Overseas: Educational Advisers and Guidance Counselors.) Because alumni are your information disseminators, you may want to prepare a contact list and put it on your web site or place it in your catalog. Be sure to get their permission to print phone numbers and e-mail addresses.

Interviews and Evaluations. The use of alumni in this area varies. Some schools prefer to standardize interviews by having their admission personnel conduct them. Others train their alumni to interview overseas. Some schools will put applicants in contact with an alumni admission representative if they request an interview; others will have the alumni admission representative contact applicants after an initial review of their application by the admission committee. Some admission officers have alumni ask very specific questions and provide very sophisticated forms for their feedback, all communicated via e-mail. It is a curious phenomenon, but many times alumni are the most critical reviewers and provide the strongest opinions to the admission committee.

Assisting Institutional Representatives. As previously mentioned, alumni can help by giving visiting institutional representatives valuable cultural, economic, and educational information about their country. They can also help with logistics by suggesting the best locations for events, directions to schools, and the most effective means of advertising your visit.

Predeparture Reception. Local alumni can help prepare new students to leave for study at your school. Having experienced the anxiety international students feel before departure, and armed with a sense of the information students need, alumni are excellent presenters at predeparture events.

The foregoing activities are just a sampling of how you can use alumni in international student recruitment. They require different degrees of effort and levels of sophistication and budgeting. Their effectiveness may not be determined by their sophistication, however, as one-time activities such as the predeparture send-off may have modest budgetary implications but an enormous benefit to incoming students.

Keep alumni informed about student applicants from their area. Tell them who was admitted and who enrolled. Their relationship with students can evolve as you progress through the admission cycle: from a provider of basic information and admission materials to a mentor as the student prepares for departure. Alumni may also appreciate an annual list of other international alumni admission representatives, and you may wish to create a listserv to allow them to share their experiences.

Be an advocate for your alumni and for strong alumni office programming and support. Remember that a relationship developed among your alumni in their home countries can be strong advertising. Prospective applicants may be impressed with the camaraderie your alumni have developed and the pride they have in their school.

Be sure to say *thank you*. One of the most important contributions international alumni can make is an introduction of your school to future students. Be sure your campus officials recognize this as a valuable contribution and recognize the international alumni for their contributions, no matter how large or small.

Resource Networks Overseas: Educational Advisers and Guidance Counselors

EDUCATIONAL ADVISERS in U.S. consulates, binational centers, and other facilities around the world are the first point of contact for many prospective international students seeking information on higher education in the United States. A prospective student's interest can run the gamut from a short-term training opportunity to a doctoral degree. The adviser provides unbiased and current information that will allow the student to make an informed choice about education in the United States. To be effective, advisers must have comprehensive knowledge of the U.S. educational system and of the educational system of the students they serve.

Educational advisers are a diverse group who live and work overseas for public and private organizations. They can be American, host-country nationals, or nationals from other countries. Many have studied or traveled in the United States; others may have earned degrees locally and have never been "stateside." Most advisers are full- or part-time employees or volunteers whose sole responsibility is to advise prospective students about U.S. higher education. Some advisers perform multiple roles, serving as librarians, testing coordinators, or even as teachers in local universities or language schools.

Advisers work in educational advising centers, which are located in most world capitals and every major city. The Department of State (DOS), through its Advising, Teaching, and Specialized Programs Division, assists more than 400 centers by providing various levels of funding for items such as reference books, computer equipment, salaries, and professional training and development. The educational advising centers supported by DOS do not charge a fee for basic information services; however, they may charge fees for individualized services, such as one-on-one advising or assisting visiting college representatives with local arrangements. Advising centers may also be supported by private organizations and local governments.

Advisers play an important public relations role in their local communities, interpreting U.S. education for the host government. Advisers often come into contact with ministry officials who may sponsor training programs designed to produce a flow of new expertise into the host country. They can act as liaisons with local English-language schools, professional organizations (for such things as in-country licensing), finance officials, and the media. Advisers also must keep abreast of economic and academic trends among the population they serve. They use their expertise to identify popular fields and levels of study, the regions of the United States that are most attractive to their students, and the financial forecast for prospective students from their countries.

Worldwide educational advisers share a common goal and commitment to represent U.S. higher education, yet their operating environments vary significantly from country to country and often, within a single country, from city to city. Some advising centers are quite modern, with the latest computer equipment and communications capabilities. Others are small and underequipped, with limited capabilities to communicate with the rest of the world. Some centers have facilities for group counseling sessions and expansive libraries; others can be one-person operations. Many centers operate in busy commercial areas; others may be in secure locations that require visitors to be screened. Overall, most of the advising centers are busy operations, often in spite of their sizes or resources.

The profession of overseas educational advising has grown tremendously in recent years, largely because of the advent of computer technology. It has removed the isolation previously experienced by many advisers and serves as a catalyst to growing networks among the advisers and U.S. admission offices. The World Wide Web, in particular, has accelerated the flow of information about study in the United States.

WHERE OVERSEAS ADVISING CENTERS CAN BE FOUND

- **United States Information Service Posts**
  These centers, part of the U.S. embassy, offer educational advising services, either on a full- or part-time basis.

- **Binational Centers**
  With a mandate to foster mutual understanding between the citizens of the United States and those of the host country, binational centers often offer advising as an adjunct service to English instruction.

- **Fulbright Commission Offices**
  The responsibilities of these offices are very broad, including sponsoring seminars and workshops and offering orientation programs for Fulbright grantees. Within this mandate, some commissions offer educational advisory services.

- **Overseas Offices of U.S.-Based International Organizations**
  America-Middle East Educational & Training Services (AMIDEAST), the Institute of International Education (IIE), the International Research and Exchanges Board (IREX),

Educational advisers in each region of the world organize and participate in professional development conferences and workshops for new and experienced advisers, some of which are sponsored by DOS. Advisers in Europe, for example, hold a major professional conference every three years for both advisers and U.S. admission representatives.

International School Guidance Counselors

Advisers, however, are not the only sources of information on U.S. higher education for international students. A savvy admission representative will also be well served by working with guidance counselors from international schools.

In almost every major city of the world, an admission representative will find an "international school"—an independent, nonprofit school that offers a U.S. college preparatory curriculum. International schools—some well-known and long-established and others new and rapidly growing—serve a diverse student population composed of U.S. citizens, host-country nationals, and third-country nationals. The students attending these schools may be the dependents of foreign service personnel, international business representatives, expatriates, or from the host-country population. Many international schools offer a dual curriculum to meet the needs of their widely divergent student bodies, offering not only a U.S. high school diploma (typically with honors and advanced-placement courses) but also the host country's secondary school curriculum or an International Baccalaureate Diploma program.

and the American Council of Teachers of Russian (ACTR) are examples of organizations whose responsibilities may include advising individuals as well as placing them in U.S. education institutions on behalf of government or corporate sponsors.

- **Foreign Governments, Universities, and Private Local Organizations**
  Examples of these are the Bangkok Bank; Services Communs Universitaires d'Information et d'Orientation or Joint University Information Services (SCUIO) centers at French universities; the Venezuelan-American Friendship Association (AVAA) in Caracas, the Soros Foundation and Open Society Institute, and the advising centers operated by the government of the People's Republic of China. ∎

Source: Adapted from Deupree, John, and Theresa Carroll Schweser. 1994. "Overseas Educational Advisers. A Worldwide Resource." In *The Admission Strategist* 21, Fall.

International schools operate autonomously but generally adhere to or exceed established educational standards and practices in the United States. Most of the independent American-style schools overseas are accredited by one of the regional accrediting associations in the United States.

Another important group of overseas schools are the Department of Defense Dependents Schools (DoDDS), which are supported by the Department of Defense Education Activity (DoDEA). This school system for children in kindergarten through grade 12 is similar to a state education system or a large city school system. The parents of its students are drawn from all branches of the military and include civilian personnel. The system is highly centralized, with headquarters at DoDEA, in Washington, DC. According to the DoDEA mission statement, "Courses of study in DoDDS schools parallel those found in public schools in the United States. Students vary in ethnic and racial backgrounds and in heritage as widely as the U.S. regions from which they come." DoDDS schools are accredited by the North Central Association of Schools and Colleges. In 1998, DoDDS operated 51 high schools in 14 countries, located in Europe, the Pacific, and the Americas (Panama and Cuba).

A significant majority of graduates from the international schools are not U.S. citizens, but are U.S.-college bound. This well-educated, highly motivated student population is served, in most schools, by a college admission guidance counselor. Many of these counselors are professionally trained U.S. citizens; others, however, paralleling their advising center colleagues, are host- or third-country citizens. In overseas schools assisted by the State Department, the ratio in 1995 of seniors to counselors averaged 43:1 worldwide. The ratios ranged from an average of 26:1 in the Near East and South Asia to 76:1 in East Asia.

Depending on the size and location of an international school, the college admission counselor often plays more than one role. International schools located in major cities frequently have large student bodies that demand a multiperson counseling staff with an individual dedicated to counseling a specific group of students. In smaller schools, however, the college counselor may work with multiple grades and also serve as a curriculum director, a teacher, a test center supervisor, or even an administrator.

College counselors work in diverse school environments, as do their advising colleagues. Many of the international schools throughout the world are on the cutting edge of technology, providing a wired building that gives students and counselors access to the Internet and the World Wide Web, and therefore to college and university web sites or e-mail around the globe. But other schools do not yet enjoy all the benefits that technology can offer. Because of local restrictions, a school may have, for example, only one Internet connection that must be shared by all administrators.

At the same time, college counselors in the international schools have a strong and growing network to support their professional development. Each region of the world is served by a regional school association, which acts as a central professional organization for the school's administrators, faculty, and counselors. Many of these regional associations, such as the European Council of International Schools (ECIS), hold annual conferences that not only draw counselors from throughout the region but sometimes significant numbers of U.S. admission representatives as well. At the same time, overseas counselors are increasingly participating in stateside professional associations and summer training opportunities. A division of the National Association for College Admission Counseling (NACAC), the Overseas Association of College Admission Counselors (OACAC), meets twice a year in the United States, once after the NACAC national conference in the fall and once in the summer.

Establishing Relationships with Advisers and Counselors

In working with overseas educational advisers and international school college counselors, follow these general guidelines:

- Establish trust between your institution and advisers and counselors.

- Respect the advisers' and counselors' positions.

- Become a resource for the advisers and counselors with whom you work.

Establish Trust

Advisers and counselors thrive on learning about positive student experiences at U.S. colleges and universities they have recommended—and the word spreads quickly among students. Advisers and counselors want to know that your programs will meet their students' needs and that your campus has services in place to support them once they arrive. The single most important thing that a U.S. institution can do is to deliver what is promised. Remember that students' negative impressions or experiences circulate through informal networks as well.

Advisers and counselors want to know that you are serious in your outreach to the students they represent. For example, counselors in international schools complain that too many U.S. institutions send applications developed for foreign students to American students abroad. A 1995 survey of guidance counselors in international schools supported by the U.S. Department of State revealed that State Department-assisted schools, "the most frequently stated suggestions for improved relationships with U.S. colleges focused on the need to provide more opportunities to meet directly with the college officials, for colleges to send their application materials, and for colleges to send videos."

Establish procedures at your institution to address the diversity inherent in international schools. As one educational adviser has shared, "My contacts with admission representatives from U.S. institutions have changed the nature of advising in our center. We are much more current, responsive, and efficient." Whenever possible, visit advising centers and international schools. Establish regular communications with these two professional groups through such means as web sites, e-mail, mailings, conferences, or Internet discussion groups.

An important resource for contacting educational advisers is the *Directory of Overseas Educational Advising Centers,* published by the College Board. The advisers' networks can be accessed on the World Wide Web through NAFSA's web site at http://www.nafsa.org/oseas/. The ECIS directory and the annual *Directory of Overseas Schools* published by the International Schools Services (ISS) in Princeton, N.J., are important references to add to every recruiter's shelf. Additionally, each of the regional school associations publishes directories of its member schools; many U.S. institutions are associate members of these organizations.

Respect the Advisers' and Counselors' Positions

Institutional representatives need to acknowledge the difficulties that advisers and counselors face when planning visits, mailings, or contacts. Advisers and counselors usually welcome visits by college and university representatives, but they understandably prefer visits planned in advance. Remember that educational advisers often fill multiple roles. Similarly, in many schools, counselors work with students on college admission in addition to teaching, developing the curriculum, and providing general counseling services. Unsolicited mailings are another consideration; learn the customs regulations of different countries. An advising center or school library may want your materials but not be able to afford a significant customs fee to process an incoming package. Overseas counselors in the 1995 survey stated that "college catalogs, college viewbooks, and general college guidebooks were the most influential reference materials for their students."

Become a Resource for Advisers and Counselors

Ongoing communication between institutions and the centers and schools is very important; remember that the information you provide will be shared repeatedly with students. Be ready to answer questions about the admission process and U.S. higher education in general. Put advisers and counselors in touch with other institutions similar to yours. When you visit an advising center or an international school, ask how you can be a resource to students and parents. You may often be viewed as an expert on U.S. higher education and so can reinforce the work of the advisers and counselors.

A new resource for overseas educational advisers, *Advising for Study in the United States: A Manual for Educational Advising Professionals* (The College Board 1998), succinctly lists ways in which institutional representatives can support an advising center or an international school when making a visit:

- Organize an information workshop for advisers, volunteers, or counselors.

- Provide in-house training on a specific topic, such as a specific field of study, or transfer students, particularly for new or volunteer advising staff.

- Give a presentation to students at the advising center on specific topics, such as writing application essays, how colleges and universities make admission decisions, financial aid for graduate students, or popular fields of study.

- Offer an evening lecture to the parents of prospective students.

- Talk to preselected students.

- Review the center's handouts, answer advisers' questions, provide advice on organizing the center or materials, or assist with technology (elicit opinions on using the Internet, computer search programs, etc.).

- Set up a booth to publicize the advising center and its services at overseas fairs and other events in which you may be participating.

- Visit a ministry of education, new institution, or the U.S. Information Service (USIS) post.

- Provide specific university materials, such as application forms, departmental information, videos, CD-ROMs, and pennants.

- Bring publications that may be difficult to obtain outside the United States.

- Provide updates on topical educational issues in the United States.

- Bring news and concerns of students from the host country currently on campus.

- Depending on the time of year, provide assistance with predeparture or reentry orientation.

- Share news about graduates who are returning to the host country and recommend names of those who could be of assistance in predeparture or reentry programs.

A unifying theme among the advisers and counselors is their desire to establish solid working relationships with U.S. admission representatives—and to see the students they advise and counsel well placed at American colleges and universities.

Working with Third-Party Recruiters and Agents

THIS CHAPTER EXAMINES the use of third-party recruiters and agents. For purposes of the chapter, third-party recruiters are defined as people who are not regular employees of the college or university that they represent and are compensated by a university for the specific purpose of recruiting international students for that institution. Agents are representatives of and are compensated by students or groups of students who are seeking admission to a U.S. college or university. Agents may approach the U.S. institutions to "sell" their clients or college representatives may approach agents to sell their institutions so the agents will refer students to those universities.

In the United States, many international education professionals believe that using third-party recruiters or agents to recruit international students is a sign of weakness or poor practice. This attitude reflects a limited perspective and may sell our colleagues short. In aggressive recruitment programs, colleges may need to employ people outside the staff to cover the vast international marketplace. And, the nature of agents abroad is changing. Increasingly, people in other countries are seeing professional educational advising as a worthwhile and needed service. In some countries, it is common practice for prospective students to use agents or agencies when seeking placement in a foreign university. One successful agency in Japan advises students on education in the United States, Canada, Australia, and Europe.

Under the proper circumstances, contracting with third parties to represent your university is ethical as long as the recruiter is trained and the representation is consistent with good recruitment practices and the ethical principles enunciated by NAFSA. NAFSA's basic standards and policies may be found on the association's web site. There is also nothing wrong with forming relationships with agents once they have been screened, their references checked, and the quality of students they represent identified. As long as you are willing and able to carefully screen the people with whom your institution does business, there is no reason to refuse, as a matter of policy or principle, to work with third-party recruiters or agents. However, third-party recruiters and agents should be used only in concert with, or as part of, a well-developed international recruitment plan monitored by on-campus staff.

Some third-party recruiters live in the United States and some live and work in the country or region in which they recruit. Soliciting referrals, making introductions, identifying new sources of prospective students, performing specific services, and recruiting students are some of the activities performed by third-party recruiters. The work is similar to that of full-time employees, but the compensation is usually different. Some universities make unofficial arrangements, usually verbal, while some issue letters of understanding or written contracts. Third-party recruiters should be required to have the same credentials and skills as the full-time admission staff.

In some countries, the term "agent" is being replaced by "study-abroad adviser," much like the titles used in the United States. Although agents abroad typically operate outside of the institutional environment, they are nonetheless interested in offering a credible and successful service. They must face parents and returning students, and if their placements turn out poorly, their reputation, and consequently their business, will suffer. Because advising is usually provided for a fee, the success of the business depends on appropriate placements.

Agents' credentials vary as widely as the services they perform and their status within the institution. In some countries, agents have their own organizations and networks and are developing professional standards.

Most agents have an interest in doing a reputable job of learning about U.S. education and your institution, and advising the student competently. Some, however, may really be running a travel agency and offer advising merely to get prospective travelers into the travel office. Some referral agents act on behalf of commercial language schools that have promised to assist their students in finding a degree program. Among these groups, too, one finds good and bad agents.

Who Uses Third-Party Recruiters and Why?

Two commonly stated but not universally accepted reasons for using third-party recruiters are cost-effectiveness and maintaining enrollment levels. Most institutions cannot afford to recruit in all markets simultaneously or in the variety of countries from which they wish to receive students. Using third-party recruiters has proved beneficial for institutions that give the practice adequate thought, establish cogent guidelines, and treat third-party recruiters as contract employees.

When an institution has experienced a decline in enrollment, with attendant budget problems, international students are one of several audiences that may be targeted for increasing enrollment. Likewise, when a campus is "internationalizing" or "globalizing," international student enrollment may be identified as an institutional priority. In such circumstances, an institution may consider using a third-party recruiter in conjunction with other regular international recruitment activities to increase or stabilize its enrollments from certain parts of the world. In addition, the university may wish to diversify enrollment. Enrolling too many students from one country has disadvantages, and it is prudent to vary the countries of enrollment. Using third-party recruiters may be the most effective way to diversify.

Who Uses Agents and Why?

The best, most productive long-term recruitment is done by full-time university staff operating from the campus. For the prospective student, there is no substitute for the quality of contact with a well-trained, full-time campus representative. However, many institutions—public and private; large and small; undergraduate, graduate, and professional—use agents. English as a second language (ESL) programs, general studies programs, and summer sessions are part of the mix as well. Some institutions qualify or disguise their relations with agents. Within a given institution, some schools or programs may use agents whereas others may not. The admission office, for example, may be more reluctant to use (or acknowledge use of) agents than is the ESL program, where faster turnover and more explicit revenue targets make continuous recruitment a necessity. In some ESL programs, 40 percent of a semester's enrollments come via agents.

In addition to representing local students, agents may also represent your institution overseas. They function in a different way from third-party recruiters in that they usually work for multiple entities at once, connecting students with universities, universities with students, representing the interest of parents, and so on while third-party recruiters usually represent only one university at a time. Agents can help you recruit on several fronts at once. They may have contracted to represent your programs specifically, whereas advisers at the educational information centers discussed in the previous chapter may not represent one institution over another.

Agents living in the target country know the local environment better than recruiters who visit occasionally. Such agents become a continuous presence in the environment and represent the institution year-round. Most institutional representatives are limited to making a short visit once or twice a year, thereby missing many recruitment opportunities. An agent can provide information to students on an on-going basis and supply the institution with leads throughout the year. However, an agent's scope of authority to act on behalf of the university must be clearly defined and monitored.

Disadvantages of Using Agents

If you use an agent to locate your students, what are you missing or what can go wrong? If not done right, using an agent can become a public-relations nightmare. One or two misunderstandings may hurt your institution's reputation for years to come.

Using agents can be more expensive than anticipated and the costs may be hard to contain. Weigh the costs of agent-based recruiting against the cost and advantages of regular international recruitment activities conducted by campus staff or contracting with a third-party recruiter who will represent your institution at all times while overseas.

Reasons not to use agents include the following:

- You will not learn as much about the local educational, cultural, economic, or social environment of target regions if you do not visit regularly. Understanding the environment of your recruits is just as important internationally as it is domestically.

- Unless agents are on campus to learn of ongoing changes in academic programs, deadlines, or requirements, they may give students incorrect information. Regular contact via the Internet can help solve this problem.

WHAT AGENTS CAN AND CANNOT DO

Agents can:
- Distribute your materials on a regular basis to local candidates.
- Place advertising in local papers on your behalf, particularly in the local language.
- Give you advice on what majors local students are currently seeking.
- Assist you in finding in their countries sources of students in underrepresented majors.
- Arrange appointments for you when you visit.
- Gather students for you to see when you visit.
- Learn about your certificate, diploma, and degree programs and admission requirements and represent you in the local environment.

Agents cannot:
- Make admission decisions or promise admission to particular programs.
- Issue Immigration and Naturalization Service (INS) and Department of State (DOS) forms needed by students to obtain a U.S. visa.
- Collect money from the student for tuition and fees.
- Overstate or misrepresent their authority on your behalf. ∎

- Agents may make promises you cannot deliver. Local cultural and political pressures may cause agents to overstate what they can deliver. You must be sure that agents understand the limits of their authority.

- Agents may be tempted to commit fraud. They may, for example, overstate the cost of attending your institution, collect the money, and retain the difference between the amount owed and the amount collected. Worse, they may abscond with the whole amount. It is not a good idea to allow agents to collect tuition and fees on your behalf. Insist that, as soon as the referral is made, you communicate directly with the student.

- It is difficult to monitor the day-to-day behavior of agents. They may perform their duties in a manner that is not consistent with the behavior you expect of people associated with your institution. Doing so could hurt your institution's reputation.

- Agencies may expect quick service for their clients and additional attention once the student arrives. In return for favors granted, the agency may ask for the university's help in placing an unqualified son or daughter of an important family. Understand the culture in which your agents operate and plan ahead for the difficulties caused by cultural differences.

- Agents may ask to be your "exclusive representative" in a given city or country. The agency may spend money promoting the university and want credit for eventual placements even if it did not refer them personally. Agents may use their relationship with your institution in their promotional materials. Although doing so may be desirable under certain circumstances, caution is advised. Know how enrolled students were referred to you, and be clear about the circumstances under which a referral fee is payable.

Finding a Reliable Agent to Represent Your Institution

It is easy to find eager agents wishing to represent you, but it is not easy to find a good one who knows his or her business and will represent you competently. If you wish to use agents to recruit international students, you must invest the time required to find a reputable agency.

Referral agents may appear when you least expect them. They may visit your campus to learn more about your institution. Spend some time with them when they are on your campus. You may also encounter prospective agents at professional conferences and international college fairs. Be ready with criteria and questions.

You may have to seek out an agent. If you have particular target countries in mind, it may be worthwhile to visit them to locate an agent. The advantage of meeting agents in this way is that you can see their place of business, see how they present other universities, check out computer facilities, and query them at length on their knowledge of U.S. higher education and your institution. You should also seek local references. Local counselors and advisers may be able to make introductions and help you narrow the field.

International Conferences, Exhibitions, and Fairs (ICEF) sponsors workshops that bring together educational advisers, referral and travel agents, and university representatives, but not students. The workshops are held in locations such as Miami, for South American contacts, and Hawaii, for Asian contacts.

Engaging an Agent

Begin by seeking the advice of those who have the most experience with agents. Consult sister institutions to find a knowledgeable person with experience in a target country of interest to you.

Managing agents requires a lot of time. An effective recruitment program requires that you not only respond to your agents' communications but that you guide and direct their activities so that you get needed results. Managing agents can consume other resources: costs for services such as international telephone calls and faxes, computer access, and mailing costs can add up. Be sure to budget for these items.

Prioritize the countries from which you wish to seek students but to which you cannot send campus-based representatives. Limit the number of countries in which you use an agent to minimize management time and reduce the risk of a negative incident resulting from insufficient oversight.

Contract only with agents whom you have met and whose qualifications and references you have checked. Ask prospective agents for references from other institutions they represent and from students whom they have placed.

Identify the number of other institutions for whom your prospective agents are working. What would make them refer a student to your institution over another institution or to another institution over yours?

Know the local labor laws for each country in which you are hiring personnel. Some countries may have labor regulations quite different from those of the United States. If you offer employment to someone there, are you subject to that country's laws? In one case an individual was employed for 12 months by a U.S. university; that country's law required that the university keep that person as an employee for life.

Be clear about how money is to be handled. Do not authorize your representatives to collect money on your behalf, but realize that such a restriction may be hard to control, particularly if you do not have a formal contract with the representative. Do everything possible to ensure that students or their families remit tuition payments directly to your institution. At the very least, make sure students know the amount of tuition and fees required for enrollment. In the absence of specific contractual arrangements, you have little control over what agents charge; without full disclosure your institution may be vulnerable to bad publicity. Students have appeared at institutions claiming to have paid tuition to an agent who cannot be found. If collection of money is involved, be sure an audit trail is in place.

An exception to the preceding rule may be made when agents have recruited a group of students to travel together to your institution. Under such circumstances, require the agents to differentiate clearly between their fees, your institution's tuition and fees, travel expenses, and other costs.

Specify how your representatives will promote their relationship with your institution. Require them to send you all printed materials that mention your

---

TIPS ON INTERNATIONAL CONTRACTS WITH FOREIGN REPRESENTATIVES

When signing contracts with agencies that may wish to represent your institution overseas, there are many things to keep in mind. The list that follows is by no means complete, but it will raise your awareness of items to be considered before the contract is written.

- The term "agent" may imply a degree of contractual legal authority that goes beyond what you wish to grant. You may wish to find a term that does not imply such authority and require that the individuals who represent you overseas use that term in introductions. "Representative" may be less authoritative.

- Take care to specify and delimit the ability of your representatives to make legally binding commitments on behalf of your institution. Otherwise, you may find yourself responsible for your representative's purchases.

- The contract should spell out in detail what the agent is and is not to do. For example, agents may disseminate your brochures and catalogs; pass the client name to you; advise the client on application procedures, registration procedures, fee structure, program content, and registration dates. Agents must not promise or imply that they can secure admission to degree programs and should not handle the completed application, receive the application fee, or collect tuition.

- What are your institution's responsibilities in the contract? How often will you provide refreshed data? In what quantities will you provide information? How should the agent secure more of your literature? How frequently will you contact the agent?

- Agree on how referrals will be identified and at what point you pay for them. Ideally, you should obligate yourself to pay only for enrollees, and not for lists of names or for applicants.

university, including advertisements, during the life of the contract. Have these translated yourself in addition to reviewing the translation supplied by the representatives. Ask to see previous representation materials—evidence that the agent successfully represented other universities.

Meet with agents annually, either on your campus or in their country. Encourage them to visit your campus as often as possible, at your expense or theirs, so they can describe to prospective students the environment, academic programs, and people. Agents will represent you much more competently from first-hand experience rather than from information gleaned from a book.

Provide agents with training about your programs, procedures, and policies. Keep them supplied with current materials. As far as possible, treat them as members of your staff who need regular communication.

Call agents several times per year to develop your relationship, inquire after their business, and assess the prospects for referrals to your programs.

- Make sure the contract can be terminated at your discretion at any time. Be sure the contract's termination clause specifies the residual obligations of the representative; for example, to return materials and equipment, prepare final reports, pay outstanding bills and taxes, remit financial statements, and so on.

- Specify the level of training you will provide for your representatives. How often will the agent receive training and at whose expense? Who will provide it and where?

- Be sure to identify any reimbursable expenses in the contract.

- Specify the equipment you expect agents to have and assign responsibility for related bills (such as telephone bills, Internet access, and computer supplies).

- Establish marketing targets and set priorities. Will the agent market intensive English programs first? Master degrees over bachelor degrees? Diplomas over certificates? Spell out what will happen if the agent does not meet your goals. Will he or she receive partial payment for goals partially met or be terminated if not successful? Be sure the contract is clear.

- Specify the nature, frequency, and form of the reports you require from the agent. By what means will reports be transmitted? Identify the consequences of failure to deliver promised reports.

- Before contracting with an agent located in another country, speak to some of your colleagues who have used agents to get more suggestions. Everyone has a good "agent tale" to tell. Learn as much as you can before signing the contract. Have the contract reviewed by a lawyer in the agent's country. A contract executed in the United States may not be binding. ■

Make e-mail a requirement for working with you. Insist that agents be accomplished in its use.

Use a database to monitor the terms of contracts made with agents. If a standard agreement is not used and a contract is crafted for the individual country or agent's circumstances, have the contract reviewed by knowledgeable legal representatives.

Establish a system for tracking referrals from agents to eliminate or at least minimize conflicts over compensation. If you cannot produce information from your system about how many referrals you received from an agent, you will have difficulty resolving disagreements over compensation. Computer monitoring will help you assess the success of the contract. If an agent produces no results, the database will help determine when it is time to make a change.

Compensating Agents

Compensation for agents varies greatly. Most referring agents are being compensated for services by the prospective student. Advising for a fee is a common practice in proprietary counseling centers abroad.

Contracts with agents should specify how the agent will be paid (in U.S. dollars or local currency, by check, or by bank transfer) and how often. Make sure you know whether your institution will incur a U.S. or foreign tax liability.

If you must pay an agent in his or her own currency, be sure someone on your staff is familiar with exchange rates and monetary exchange procedures. Someone in the office should monitor the exchange rate fluctuations, as they can greatly affect your budget. Ask your bank how to make a wire transfer, and consider establishing an account in an international bank for the agent so you can deposit money directly to his or her account. Establish a reserve for currency fluctuations.

Many public institutions in the United States are prevented by law from contracting with individuals outside the United States (or outside their state, for that matter) without layers of permission. Under such circumstances, where it is not practical to negotiate a contract for the small amount of money involved, a prospective agent may suggest that compensation should take the form of payment of expenses such as those for the agent's travel or ads the agent places that will also benefit the university. An agent may propose to make referrals to an institution, for example, in exchange for assistance in placing a particular student in a particular program, hosting a dignitary, or, indeed, hosting the agent during U.S. travel. Institutions are advised to negotiate such arrangements with care. A good, solid relationship built over years between the agent and institutional representatives can work quite well.

Some institutions retain agents by offering a certain amount of money over a certain period of time to locate qualified individuals, without specifying a precise number of students to be recruited. Such retainer arrangements ease the pressure of "head-count" compensation and place the emphasis on finding qualified individuals. If the applications you receive are insufficient in quality or quantity, the retainer is not renewed. Under retainer arrangements, agents perform a specific job for the institution within certain parameters and with certain expected outcomes.

Some institutions agree to pay agents a percentage of the tuition paid to the university. If this arrangement is chosen, determine whether the agent gets paid for subsequent semesters of enrollment or just for the first. Another model is compensation for the number of students recruited. Both models require careful definition; both are ripe for scams. Agents operating under such arrangements may be motivated to seek head count rather than qualified students. Institutions are cautioned to specify the exact conditions for payment (e.g., upon the student's enrollment). If the institution does not do so, it can expect frivolous applications and troublesome claims from the agents who generated them.

Compensation based on the number of students recruited is not the best practice. In most cases, a flat fee for specified services is more desirable as long as you can ascertain that satisfactory progress is being made. Paying a fee per student may allow another institution to get the better students from a given crop. Specify how you will determine when the student has been successfully recruited. How long must the student study with you before you compensate the agent? one week? one term? one semester? What happens to the agency fee if the student drops out and gets a refund of tuition? If the agency has collected the tuition and paid the fees, who gets the refund?

When compensation is arranged, are there layers of reward to be earned? Should agents receive the same compensation for each enrollment, or should they be paid on a graduated scale? Should you require a minimum number of enrollments before any fees are due? Will you provide a bonus for extraordinary results?

In the past, NAFSA helped U.S. institutions identify qualified agents and agencies—those who were knowledgeable about U.S. higher education. With grant money, the association maintained a file of agents' profiles. Although it is no longer feasible to maintain such profiles, the form NAFSA used may be useful in screening agencies. See appendix G for a copy of the questionnaire.

Many institutions report satisfactory arrangements with agents abroad. Success is usually proportional to planning, management, communication, and commitment. The best relationships are built on trust, respect, and competence. After careful selection, incorporate the representatives as part of your on-going recruitment planning and let them know that you are interested in a long-term relationship.

Special Considerations

Intensive English Programs

A WELL-CONCEIVED PLAN results in the most effective marketing initiatives. This is particularly true for the intensive English program (IEP). Marketing is far too expensive to be pursued haphazardly or in reaction to sudden downturns in regional economies. An effective marketing plan enables IEPs to anticipate market changes by having clear targets and allocating specific resources to stated goals. For example, when a program reaches a certain threshold percentage of a country or language group, advertising, travel, or mailing dollars can be redistributed to less well-represented, but promising new markets. In this way, the IEP becomes less vulnerable to shifts in student demographics.

IEPs have been particularly susceptible to wild enrollment swings precisely because few have developed and adhered to sound marketing plans. Instead, they too often have become dependent on the fleeting policies of foreign governments. Over the years huge influxes of students have come suddenly from various countries: Venezuelan and Iranian students arrived in the late 1970s; Saudi Arabian, Chinese, and Malaysian students in the early 1980s; and Japanese, Turkish, Thai, and Korean students in the 1990s. This succession of enrollees meant that enrollments remained steady or even increased for many programs, with IEP directors growing quietly complacent and perhaps even congratulating themselves for their "astute planning."

In reality, their marketing approach was more passive than proactive. A proactive plan actively cultivates new markets. Doing so enables the program to sustain enrollment levels and achieve a truly diverse student body, despite fluctuations in regional economies or changes in government policy. A marketing plan that is frequently revisited and updated keeps administrators vigilant against "enrollment creep" by any one nationality.

Be True to Your Mission

Begin developing your marketing plan by reviewing or revising your IEP's mission statement. Don't try to reinvent your program, but rather reflect accurately on the philosophy and core values of the IEP. If the IEP remains grounded in its mission, program administrators will avoid temptations to pursue programs not in line with the IEP's stated objectives, to make promises they cannot fully honor, or to adopt a marketing strategy that is contrary to its own corporate convictions or that of its host institution. A mission statement has integrity. It is a vision to which an organization must remain true. Marketing can either enhance or compromise the reputation of an IEP to the extent it remains true to the institution's mission.

Ask Yourself Some Questions

Once program administrators have defined the IEP's mission, they can then formulate a marketing plan that exploits the IEP's strengths and targets a specific clientele. The following questions will help an IEP's marketing committee begin to draft a promising plan:

- What are the unique strengths of your IEP, host institution, and location? Ask students regularly why they chose your program and what they like best after having studied for a session or two.

- What policy or procedural changes might make your program more marketable? Consider placing your application online to make it easier for students to apply; lobby for a conditional admission policy, particularly at the graduate level; review your session start dates to see if your calendar might be adjusted to better coincide with the holiday schedules of your target markets; and consider enhanced orientation services for new students, such as airport pick-up or expanded homestay and dormitory programs.

- What underrepresented countries appear to be promising markets? Consult *Open Doors*, the Institute of International Education's annual international student census, for enrollment trends; consider individual and institutional contacts your program or other departments might have in specific countries; and recruit graduate or undergraduate interns to conduct market research on specific countries.

- What is your enrollment target? Consider number of students and demographic factors.

- What human and financial resources are available for marketing? Propose cost-sharing advertising or fair expenses with the admission office; consider the true opportunity cost involved in recruiting trips; and lobby for a specific marketing budget if you don't already have one.

- How will the effectiveness of current or prospective brochures, advertisements, advertising sites, web pages, fairs, and recruiting agents be determined? Track inquiries and applications to determine their sources; use student and alumni focus groups to assess the quality of advertisements, web pages, and brochures.

- What is a reasonable timeline for achieving the marketing objective? Set immediate, intermediate, and long-term goals for each phase of your plan; develop a process for reassessing or revising your plan at each stage of the timeline. (See chapter 2.2, Creating a Strategic Plan.)

Get to Work

Once the basis for the program is established and the marketing plan is in place, the institution should decide which specific marketing activities it can do well, which ones promise return on the investment, and which ones can meet the budget constraints. The most successful marketing plan is broadly defined and includes some of the suggested activities described below. These techniques, in various combinations, have produced increased enrollment for many IEP programs.

Marketing is a matter of not only sharing the message, but also of actually completing the sale by enrolling students. The program that can increase application rates by just a few percentage points will see its enrollment rise dramatically. Thus a program with a limited marketing budget may be wise to allocate funds not for efforts to increase its pool of inquiries, but for increased staff and support to maximize the applicant pool, admit, and enroll students. These activities include personalizing response letters, making follow-up phone calls, or establishing evening hours to permit potential applicants to call more conveniently during their available hours.

Publicity Materials

IEP recruitment is complicated by the likelihood that the prospective student's knowledge of English may be minimal. Preparing printed materials in the language of the country in which you plan to recruit may be necessary, and it is helpful to have a program representative who speaks the native language available in-country to provide additional information. (See chapter 4.4, Working with Third-Party Recruiters and Agents.) Information and advice available in the local language will help potential students and their families feel more confident and comfortable with the program.

In designing their promotional literature, many IEPs mistake their readers' need for simplified language for a need to limit the breadth and depth of the information provided. Do not fall into this trap. ESL clients are discriminating shoppers who look for extensive detail before selecting a program of study. Well-designed web pages can be very effective. A well-developed web page provides small amounts of information on each page, both to minimize down-load times and memory requirements and to make the information easier to absorb by potential applicants. University-based programs should make every effort to ensure a prominent, easily found link to the host institution and vice versa. (See chapter 3.2, Creating Effective Publicity Materials.)

Measuring Proficiency and Proper Placement

Convincing students with intermediate English-language skills of their need for further language training can be difficult at times. Many prospective students believe they already know English well enough to begin an academic program. An evaluation of a writing sample, as well as an oral interview, can help them recognize their true English proficiency. Showing students catalogs that indicate the level of English proficiency required for admission at a variety of colleges and universities can also be helpful in demonstrating the need for additional training. Listening to English-language tapes or reading written samples and testing the student on the content may successfully demonstrate deficiencies in English. The optimum method for determining English-language proficiency is a formal test. In some countries, it is difficult to obtain such a test and more subjective evaluations must be made.

Proper placement of students influences enrollment. Students who are placed in classes below their skill level quickly become bored. Those placed above their skill level may drop out. Proper assessment at the time of arrival, by testing and retesting, adds to the success and reputation of the program.

Program Format

The length of the IEP and the available starting dates are important recruiting points. If students and their families understand approximately how long it will take to achieve a level of proficiency necessary for admission to an academic program, they will be able to evaluate whether they can afford an extensive IEP in the United States. Some families may have saved for an academic program but may not have considered the cost of additional English-language training. The starting dates for an English-language program are also important. Students will want to complete their IEP and then begin their academic program without a costly delay.

Recruitment Techniques

University-based and non-university based IEPs sometimes use similar recruitment approaches. Both recruit via their alumni, attend fairs in many countries, send direct mailings to prospective students, and visit high schools abroad. Many programs have established networks of recruitment representatives around the world.

Joint Initiatives by University-Based Programs

University-based IEPs need not proceed alone when it comes to recruitment. In fact, limited marketing resources can be spread further and used to greater effect if leveraged with the resources of other units. The savvy admission officer will see the advantages of teaming with the IEP on campus to reach a far greater number of potential applicants. An equally savvy IEP administrator does well to negotiate an agreement with the admission office to include:

- Financial support for IEP representatives to attend overseas fairs
- Joint advertisements in selected student guides and journals
- Conditional admission requiring successful completion of the IEP in lieu of the Test of English as a Foreign Language (TOEFL)
- Joint scholarships (for ESL and undergraduate tuition)
- Publication of a joint admission brochure targeting international students and emphasizing the IEP and other appropriate college resources
- Shared mailing lists
- Training of staff from both units to be alert to opportunities for student referrals
- Shared translation resources, such as bilingual staff members, to process inquiries.

Because it is unlikely that the recruitment goals of the university admission office and the IEP will overlap completely, efforts can be focused on areas where interests intersect. Nevertheless, it is almost a certainty that ongoing interaction between the two units will broaden opportunities for cooperative initiatives.

Similar arrangements can be made with the graduate school on campus or with individual graduate programs. IEPs that have been able to obtain conditional admission agreements from popular graduate programs (such as engineering, computer science, or business administration) may be less affected by global economic downturns. Moreover, graduate departments in need of foreign teaching assistants may be delighted to have IEPs assist them in recruiting and screening qualified students with adequate oral proficiency skills, or at least those who might attain appropriate language levels after a few months of intensive ESL instruction.

Use of Third-Party Recruiters

Ten or twenty years ago, university-based programs relied heavily on recruitment by academic departments and on the reputation of their institutions. In recent years, they have followed the example of the non-university based programs in recruitment strategies. As a result, a large number of university-based programs have established a network of representatives around the world.

One of the principal differences between the recruitment techniques of these two types of programs is the payment of commissions to international representatives. Non-university based English-language programs often choose to pay commissions. The amount varies but is generally based on the tuition rate of the program. University-based programs may have restrictions established by the governing bodies of their institutions. In general, university-based programs that are part of an extension division have more flexibility than do those that belong to an academic department. Some university-based programs provide advertising allowances for the agent instead of a per-student commission. In effect, this provides the same incentive to the representative as a commission would, since a portion of the agent's commission inevitably goes to cover advertising.

International students and their families often need help in obtaining information about academic institutions, admission requirements, and costs. Some live in cities where U.S. government agencies supply such information, but many come from locations where educational advising is limited or nonexistent. Admission personnel from the United States cannot adequately cover the globe; therefore, they need to obtain the assistance of local representatives. People and organizations of high visibility and good reputation in a community can assist a university by advertising their relationship to the institution and the agents' availability for counseling.

The institution, in return, must provide continuous updates on new or revised academic programs, housing options, and tuition rates. If agents are not kept up to date, they cannot do their job properly, and students will suffer, as will the institution's reputation. Regular evaluations of the representative must be conducted to determine if the relationship should be continued or terminated. (See chapter 4.4, Working with Third-Party Recruiters and Agents.)

Fairs

Attendance at international education fairs serves multiple purposes. If the program has representatives in the country where the fair is being held, an IEP staff member may attend to assist the representatives at the fair and to evaluate their performance. Once experience is obtained, successful agents may be able to take care of future fairs alone. If the IEP does not have representation in the country, attendance at the fair not only helps to recruit new students but also gives the institution's staff a chance to locate representatives in that area. Personal contact by a staff member or trained agent coupled with quality literature about the program will enhance the chances of student enrollment. Many prospective students attend fairs for several years before they are ready to come to the United States. Some will return to the fairs in subsequent years to renew their acquaintance with the institution and to get up-to-date information. In the process of making their decision about when and where to enroll, they will have discussed their plans with their friends and may have influenced others to join them in attending the institution. (See chapter 3.4, Education Fairs.)

Retention

If an IEP can increase the average student stay from four to six months, then it has effectively increased its revenue by 50 percent without recruiting a single new student. How, then, does a program retain its current students for additional sessions? First, an IEP must involve every member of its staff in marketing. The secretary, the orientation coordinator, the faculty, and the receptionist are all important to retention.

Second, a program that relentlessly pursues excellence and improvement keeps its students longer. Investment in curriculum development, facility renovation, and technological upgrades is a shrewd form of marketing, for such efforts can lead to greater student satisfaction. A retention-based marketing plan focuses on quality that can be measured. The program that can clearly and specifically demonstrate to its students just how much progress they have made with their language development (for example, through audio, video, and written portfolio assessments that are reviewed before and after each session of study) is one that will inspire its clients to re-enroll. In short, the broader the definition of marketing an IEP holds, the greater the opportunities it will envision and achieve.

Third, the retention-oriented IEP strives to remove financial roadblocks to re-enrollment by offering incentives such as scholarships, group or spousal discounts, campus job-placement assistance, deferred payment plans, less-expensive course options, and longer vacation opportunities. It is also helpful if the IEP accepts credit cards.

Finally, the program that recruits from its own student body is one that listens to its student clients. The students may desire a special class not currently offered (such as business ESL), or there may be a need to change a teacher or roommate who is causing so much unhappiness that students are considering curtailing their stay. By listening, one might be able to suggest a policy change (for example, class start times) that could boost the morale of the entire student body.

Two-Year Colleges

THE POPULARITY OF COMMUNITY COLLEGES among international students is a relatively recent phenomenon. Initially designed to provide an educational avenue for a broad range of students, community colleges experienced rapid growth after World War II. After World War II, President Truman recognized a need to address some major concerns of Americans, especially those of minorities and the economically and socially disadvantaged. Truman believed that the way to regain the freedom and democracy for which America fought was to improve the quality of and access to higher education. Truman convened the President's Commission on Higher Education for American Democracy, or the "Truman Commission Report," in 1947. The Commission was chaired by George Zook, the founder of the American Association of Junior Colleges (now the American Association of Community Colleges [AACC]). Zook believed that a vast network of publicly supported two-year institutions should be established. These colleges, called "community colleges," would be "within the reach of most citizens, charge little or no tuition, serve as cultural centers for the community, offer continuing education for adults as well as technical and general education, be locally controlled, and be a part of their state's and the nation's system of higher education." (Vaughan 1995) Today, because they provide affordable, practical, and accessible education, community colleges have gained a following among international students as an alternative to four-year educational institutions. Because, in part, of their close ties to local businesses, an increasing number of community colleges are concerned with providing a global education and welcome the knowledge and perspective that international students bring to courses, curricula, and campus life. At suburban and rural colleges, in particular, international students promote and increase diversity on campus, and can be a cost-effective way for the college to internationalize their student body and the immediate community.

The Internationalization of U.S. Community Colleges

Community colleges represent the largest segment of higher education in the United States. Nearly 1,200 institutions enroll 10.3 million students, 5.3 million of whom are seeking a degree or certificate. Most colleges provide open access, enabling both U.S. and international students to benefit from the high-quality and low-cost courses they offer. And, based on their experience with the increasingly diverse communities they serve, community colleges are becoming more aware of the importance of global understanding.

Although community colleges were created to serve their local communities, an increasing number are actively recruiting international students. Mission statements that mention the importance of educating a globally competent citizenry are often used as the foundation for recruiting international students. As anywhere, recruitment will be more successful if it occurs within the context of a campus-wide international education program that has the support of the faculty, administration, and trustees. Because community colleges provide so much workforce training and most companies prefer employees who have international experience, the international boost that recruitment brings is easy to justify in most cases. Students need to be prepared for an increasingly interdependent world. Internationalizing the campus helps prepare all students to live and work productively in the multicultural workplace.

Diversity of Academic Programs

The diversity of programs offered by community colleges and the benefits students derive from each type of program should be stressed in marketing efforts.

Transfer Programs

The associate degree program allows international students to obtain the first two years of their postsecondary education at a community college, then

---

ACCORDING TO A NATIONAL SURVEY CONDUCTED IN 1995 BY THE AACC:

- Nearly 80 percent of the 624 responding colleges offered some type of international education program—ranging from internationalizing curricula to international contract training.

- More than 63 percent offered ESL courses—by far one of the most widespread "international" courses offered at community colleges. One reason for the popularity of ESL courses is the large influx of immigrants and international students on community college campuses in many states.

- More than 167,000 immigrants and international students were enrolled in the responding community colleges during the 1995–96 academic year.

Source: Chase, Andree and James Mahoney. 1996. *Global Awareness in Community Colleges: A Report of a National Survey.* Washington, DC: American Association of Community Colleges.

transfer to a four-year institution to obtain a bachelor's degree. This may be a particularly attractive option to international students who are uncertain about their academic plans. Students may also opt to participate in the transfer program to minimize tuition costs or because they need more individualized attention as they get accustomed to living and studying in a new environment.

Technical/Occupational Certificate Programs

Certificate programs are strong components of a community college education, and these programs are of growing interest to international students and many foreign governments. Many countries lack higher education programs that address the need for specialized training on a mass scale. There are at least 1,500 specialized technical/occupational programs offered at two-year colleges nationwide, which represent a vast reservoir of expertise available to aspiring international students. Local businesses and industries often provide internship opportunities for community college students. Such opportunities can be successfully targeted toward international students because they address the workforce needs of their home countries.

Continuing Education

Through continuing education programs, international students can compound the benefits of their U.S. education. With five million students enrolled in a wide and growing array of non credit programs at community colleges, international students can usually find courses that complement their degree studies.

Marketing a Community College Education

Because of their flexibility, community colleges have much to offer international students. Specific advantages to attending a two-year college include:

- Affordability
- Links to the local community, including businesses
- Specialized technical training

When promoting the affordability of a community college education, don't be reluctant to compare tuition and fees at your institution with those of local four-year institutions.

Let potential students know that they can be active participants in the classroom and on campus, and that professors rather than graduate students generally teach courses. Close ties with the local community offer international students opportunities to make presentations about their home countries to elementary and secondary schools, and to other community groups.

ESL programs are among the most popular courses at many community colleges, so many colleges are already poised to respond to the language-training needs of international students.

Local businesses may be in need of foreign nationals to assist them with international communications. Admission personnel can work with the business and industry liaisons on campus to make such possibilities a reality for prospective international students.

A specific point to make when marketing certificate programs is that community college faculties include many professionals with experience in high-technology industries. Instructors are able to provide their students with concrete examples from industry that translate classroom theory into real work situations. These instructors allow international students to develop contacts for future professional networking.

Challenges to Recruiting for Two-Year Programs

Despite their appeal, two-year institutions face challenges in recruiting international students. Misconceptions prevalent among Americans—for example, that students enroll in community colleges only after being refused by four-year institutions—unfortunately are shared by many outside the country. The quality, variety, and value of the programs available at two-year institutions are too great to be submerged in misperceptions. Community college staff and faculty, professional associations, and state governments should work to ensure that potential students understand the community college's true role in the American higher education system.

One alarming consequence of the bias against two-year institutions is the reluctance of many U.S. consular officers to issue student visas to individuals wishing to study at community colleges. Visa denials occur for several reasons:

- Prospective students may not know what to expect from the community college or how it articulates with four-year colleges.

- The consular official may not know the current role of community colleges in U.S. higher education.

- The consular official may think that a given applicant is not a serious student.

- Community college representatives may not be aware of the proper procedures for recruiting students, which may lead to a visa denial.

Whatever the reason, the denial of a student visa may be addressed by:

- Providing all of the documentation needed in the visa process.

- Providing student applicants with detailed information about the program in which they will enroll to enable them to explain to the consular officer how their experience will advance their larger goals and objectives. Does the applicant plan to remain in the United States and transfer to a four-year institution to obtain a bachelor's degree? Or will he or she return home to use the associate's degree for a specific vocational or occupational purpose?

- Researching trends in visa issuance at the national level and demonstrating to consular officers the success of two-year institutions in meeting domestic and international workforce goals.

Not all of the recruitment challenges are related to misperception, of course. For most international students, academic success depends on the availability of advising and other support services. International educators can access training and networking opportunities through NAFSA, which will assist them in providing quality services to students. Although there are fewer numbers of NAFSA members at two-year institutions, it is simple for a two-year institution to link with NAFSA members in their regions. An institution may do this by contacting the national NAFSA coordinator for two-year institution members. Institutions that truly want to recruit international students and reap the benefits such students bring to their institution should ensure that adequate support services are in place. (See chapter 2.1, Preparing to Recruit.)

Student housing, in particular, can be a challenge; only 33 percent of community colleges have dormitory facilities. Colleges might consider other housing options that may exist, such as extended homestays with families in the surrounding community or dormitory-style student housing provided by local four-year institutions or third parties (as is now available in New York and other large cities). Whatever the options, the college must be prepared to help international students find appropriate housing.

Strategies for Recruiting International Students

Community colleges can take several approaches to international recruitment.

Consortia Arrangements

Consortia arrangements with other two- and four-year institutions in the state or region have been used successfully by many community colleges. Where articulation agreements exist between two- and four-year institutions in a given state or region, recruiters should mention the four-year institutions to which international students might transfer to earn their bachelor's degree. Many community colleges do not have the resources to sustain an international exchange program on their own. By working with nearby colleges and universities, two-year institutions can share the costs of international programs and widen opportunities for domestic and international students alike.

For instance, the Illinois Consortium for International Studies and Programs (ICISP) enables two- and four-year institutions to provide study-abroad opportunities for their students and to submit strong proposals for international programs such as Fulbright-Hays Group Projects. Study abroad often brings returns in the form of international student recruitment.

In addition to Illinois, many other states have formed consortia arrangements in order to assist them with international programs and recruiting international students. Some of these groups include the following:

- California Community Colleges for International Education
- Colorado Consortium for International Programming
- Education for Global Learning: A Consortium of Minnesota Colleges
- Florida Collegiate Consortium for International/Intercultural Education
- New Jersey Collegiate Consortium for International/Intercultural Education
- Southern Michigan Community College Consortium for International Education
- Spokane Consortium for International Studies
- West Virginia Consortium for Faculty and Course Development in International Studies

The Southern Michigan Community College Consortium for International Education, with Kalamazoo Valley Community College leading eight other two-year institutions, has been particularly successful. Although the focus of this consortium is to enhance the internationalization of the community college curricula, several colleges shared resources to provide international exchanges and study-abroad programs. Delta College in Michigan offered exchange programs with Kenya and Japan, and Macomb Community College, also in Michigan, offered an interdisciplinary exchange program to Mexico. For additional information on the Southern Michigan Community College Consortium, a good resource is *Building Community for an Interdependent World Among Michigan Community Colleges* (Sypris et. al 1994).

Fairs

Increasing numbers of two-year colleges are attending education fairs overseas. Despite the relatively high costs of travel, regular attendance at fairs is an efficient way to establish credibility in target countries. (See chapter 3.4, Education Fairs.)

Individual Institutional Recruitment

Delaware County (PA) Community College (DCCC) administrators conducted information sessions recently in areas of the world from which they wished to recruit students, working with a multinational hotel chain to obtain space for the meetings. The information session was advertised in local newspapers. Far more potential students attended than the college could accommodate. DCCC's approach is one that could be replicated by other colleges. (See chapter 3.3, International Travel.)

Single-Country Focus

A community college in Texas sent a high-level administrator to China for three weeks to meet with 50 Chinese students who had already been admitted to the college's ESL program. Upon arriving at the U.S. embassy to obtain visas for the group, the administrator was unable to consult with the consular officer and encountered a very unhelpful embassy staff. The situation turned from bad to worse when only a handful of students were actually issued visas for study. The students who were denied visas returned to their hometowns without further indication of what their enrollment status might be.

After researching the unfortunate incident, the college's administrators determined that they should have advised the U.S. Department of State of their intentions before their recruiting trip to China. The Bureau of Consular Affairs at the State Department could have proven a valuable resource. While in-country consular officers have full authority to issue and deny visas, it is possible that State Department officials in Washington might have circumvented this occurrence by intervening with their colleagues abroad. Had the Bureau of Consular Affairs been informed of the college's plan to recruit international students from China, they could have paved the way for the administrator's and students' visit to the U.S. embassy to obtain visas. There would have been no guarantee that every student in the group would be issued a visa, but less confusion may have occurred during the recruiting venture.

Successful international student recruiters must have a thorough understanding of the regulations of the Immigration and Naturalization Service (INS) and other U.S. federal agencies. This is especially true of recruiters in countries to which students tend not to return after concluding their studies in the United States.

Thorough and Complete Communication About Academic Programs and Goals

International students wishing to study at a community college must understand and be able to explain exactly why they wish to enroll in such an institution. Community-college recruiters must ensure that the students they recruit have a clear and specific plan for their education. In particular, students must be able to explain to the U.S. consular officer what they intend to do after obtaining their associate degree. Admission officers should advise students to be prepared to answer questions about where they intend to obtain further degrees or what sort of employment they intend to seek after completing their studies.

Community Support from Business and Industry

Community colleges excel at workforce and skills training, and more and more international students are choosing these specialized programs. The admission office must make it clear to students enrolling for a certificate that they may have difficulty justifying their choice to a consular officer, who will wonder about the likelihood of the student returning home after being thoroughly trained for a skill that could be used in the United States.

Word of Mouth from Satisfied Students

International students who have benefited from a community college education tend to spread the word to others in their home countries (see chapter 4.2, Making the Most of Alumni Contacts). Because word-of-mouth advertising is so powerful and effective, successful colleges could be thrust into a position of unintentional recruitment from a specific area of the world. This could distract them from maintaining an active recruitment policy, thereby causing them to become victims of their own success and vulnerable to economic dips in the areas of the world from which their students are coming. The only solution to such a predicament is to remain true to the institution's recruitment plan (see chapter 2.2, Creating a Strategic Plan), pressing forward with recruitment efforts in underrepresented areas and becoming more selective about applications from over-represented ones.

Although a community college is certainly not the right choice for all international students, it can provide unique opportunities at a reasonable cost. More and more community colleges are recruiting international students, and as they continue to reap the benefits of having international students at their institutions, more colleges will follow suit.

Reference List

Sypris, Theo. 1995. "Building Community for an Interdependent World Among Michigan Community Colleges." In *AACC-WK Kellogg Foundation Beacon College Project 1989–1995.* (Washington, DC, American Association of Community Colleges), 44-45.

Vaughan, George B. 1995. *The Community College Story: A Tale of American Innovation.* Washington, DC: American Association of Community Colleges.

Graduate Programs

IN 1998, 43 percent of the international students studying in the United States were seeking graduate degrees. They represented 11.4 percent of the total U.S. graduate student enrollment.[1] More than 70 percent of international graduate students study in five areas: engineering (20 percent), business (17.7 percent), physical and life sciences (11.7 percent), social sciences (9.7 percent), and math and computer science (11.2 percent).[2] Detailed information on the percentage of students from a particular country who study in various disciplines is published in IIE's *Open Doors*.

In particular disciplines at some universities, international students outnumber American students. At many major research universities, graduate degree programs have come to rely heavily on international students to fill teaching and research positions, and to meet minimum course enrollments.

Although many international graduate students are funded by assistantships at U.S. colleges and universities, 65 percent receive funding from a source outside the university such as personal or family funds, their home government, or an employer. The percentage of self-funded international graduate students is lower than that of self-funded international undergraduates, but it is still high enough to make graduate recruitment a worthwhile endeavor.

Challenges in Recruiting for Graduate Programs

Few universities have planned university-wide recruitment programs for graduate students. The major reasons include (1) the generally decentralized nature of graduate program management, (2) the specialized recruitment needs of graduate departments, (3) the absence of systematic procedures that characterize the articulation between secondary and tertiary education, and (4) limited resources.

Most graduate recruitment is left to individual departments or schools, and few graduate-school representatives travel abroad, with the exception of representatives in disciplines such as business, physics, chemistry, dentistry, and music. Contacts with prospective graduate students may be made by undergraduate admission representatives while traveling to recruit undergraduate students, but such contacts are usually limited to making a referral to the graduate department. The resources that support recruitment travel typically come from the undergraduate admissions budget. Although graduate departments may be given seed money to recruit, it is usually not enough to sponsor foreign travel.

Representing graduate programs is complicated by the fact that prospective graduate students are mature people with finely focused concerns and well-defined needs, while recruiting departments seek students whose teaching and research interests match their own. Graduate students figure into department life in multiple roles: as student, member of the teaching or research staff, and potential peer. Applications are closely scrutinized because faculty invest a lot of time in each student's education and career.

In many developing countries, the push for graduate degrees is not as strong as it is in the United States, nor is a graduate degree as necessary for success. Most jobs that require a degree require only a first degree, and it is not uncommon for teaching faculty in universities to be hired with a master's degree, although that is changing with increases in the supply of more highly qualified graduates. Still, university recruiters may find stronger demand in developing countries for individuals with master's degrees than for doctoral candidates.

The Role of the Graduate School

Enrollment management and graduate recruitment at U.S. universities runs the gamut from limited central coordination to complete decentralization of all responsibility to the departments. It is rare to find recruitment, application processing, and financial aid combined into a one-stop service center as is common in undergraduate enrollment centers. Although convenient for students, such centers are less useful for graduate school faculty because admission decisions are made in departments. Faculty also may view enrollment centers as absorbing resources that could be better distributed to underfunded schools and departments. In decentralized models, on the other hand, the task of recruitment at the departmental level becomes one more burden added to the many academic issues faced by department chairs and admission committee members. When resources are limited, there seems to be no satisfactory solution.

Some entity, however, must take responsibility for planning and evaluation. The dean of the graduate school must be concerned about the quality of the graduate faculty, the school's academic programs, and the graduate students the departments attract. The dean must ensure that the courses reach their minimum enrollments, that tenured faculty have students to teach, and that money is available to attract good students to assist with teaching and research. It is in the course of such planning and evaluation exercises that the role of international graduate students comes to light. Without central planning, the institution may not attract sufficient numbers of international graduate students. The institution may be seriously handicapped without international students' presence.

Competent credential evaluation is vital at the graduate level. The campus should be sure that library resources and staff expertise are available on campus (see chapter 2.3, Building Foreign Credential Evaluation Expertise). The graduate faculty should know how a U.S. degree in a particular field will be recognized abroad. They should be aware that international students who have a U.S. degree may have to take further coursework and examinations before receiving permission to practice in their chosen fields. U.S. degrees do not automatically receive recognition abroad. If aware of the home country requirements, the faculty can help students select courses that will meet both the home country requirements and the U.S. degree requirements. Many graduate schools give small amounts of transfer credit earned for previous graduate work. This may serve to shorten the time an international student has to spend in the United States or allow the student to take a substitute course.

The Role of the Department

Most recruitment of international graduate students starts with the faculty. Faculty often correspond with colleagues overseas and with prospective students well before the normal admission cycle begins. They may have come to a decision about the student's enrollment even before a formal application has been filed. In competitive majors such as physics and chemistry, keeping abreast of the recruitment process is critical. Some faculty are very informed about the strong departments in their disciplines at foreign universities. With e-mail, faculty at U.S. universities can correspond easily with a prospective student's professors early in the process to get references. Because faculty typically play a significant role in the admission process at the graduate level, their role in making contacts with foreign colleagues and prospective students is crucial in the delicate process of attracting graduate students.

Inquiries from prospective graduate students arrive at the institution in a much different way than do undergraduate inquiries. Students may have learned about a university from their current professors or from a friend studying in the United States, from research papers, professional journals, alumni, a search letter, or through Internet searches. International graduate students, like their domestic counterparts, are usually more focused in their educational goals than are undergraduates and wish to communicate directly with the faculty to discern mutual interest and to determine whether funding will be available. Individual faculty are concerned about filling their classes and not about feeding central database information. All of these factors make it more difficult to understand the graduate student applicant pool.

Competition for the best students is keen, and negotiations for high-quality international graduate students may begin well before the expected year of enrollment. Where major funding is at stake, program deadlines fall in January so that students can be considered for teaching and research assistantships. While it is true that admission offers go out during spring and even into late summer, institutions that wish to compete for the highest-quality students must recruit actively during the fall semester, or earlier, and make offers of graduate assistantships as early as February.

Because many prospective international graduate students have earned their undergraduate degree in the United States, looking within the United States for applicants is a good strategy. As is true of American students, many international students continue at the same institution for their graduate degree, so recruiting among currently enrolled undergraduates often pays off handsomely.

Because recruitment activities for graduate students are specific to the individual disciplines, many of the functions normally performed by a central admission or enrollment service at the undergraduate level are performed at the department level for graduate students. Department staff may do mailings, collect and process applications, send preliminary admission and financial aid offers, and so on. Departments are not always allotted resources to handle such tasks, however. Institutions should consider the advantages of centralizing some of the services for graduate student admission to increase efficiency, reduce costs, and improve services. Faculty must still play an important role in the contact with prospective students, but asking them to mail and process applications is not good use of their time.

E-mail increases access to program information by students, provided someone answers the inquiries. Questions and requests that go beyond asking for an application require personal attention, and personal attention is expensive. Nevertheless, the quality and timeliness of the personal contact prospective students receive will attract them to your institution. To make answering inquiries from many different places more efficient, it may be helpful for each department and the central services offices to develop a list of frequently asked (and answered) questions for distribution on the institution's web site or for use by staff in answering inquiries. Using e-mail's automatic response feature will notify the student that the inquiry was received and will allow the receiver to distribute mail to others for personal reply.

If small departments cannot handle a high volume of inquiries, consider having the admission office, enrollment center, or other entity provide first-level responses to e-mail forwarded from the department. (Of course, the department is still the best source of information about its discipline.) Any system of responding to inquiries is better than letting the mail go unanswered, which sends a negative message to the student. If you have no way to answer e-mail inquiries, do not publish the department's e-mail address.

Services for International Graduate Students

International graduate students need the same services as undergraduates. These include visa services, ESL instruction, orientation, adjustment counseling, assistance with housing, support for spouses and children, employment, practical training, and so on. (See the discussion of campus and community services in chapter 2.1, Preparing to Recruit.)

Visa Services

Most international graduate students come to the United States on F-1 (student) visas, but a larger percent of graduates request a J-1 (exchange visitor) visa than do undergraduates (in 1996-97, 10.1 percent compared with 3.6 percent). If your institution is not authorized to issue the federal form that allows a student to obtain a J-1 visa, consider seeking approval to do so. (See chapter 2.4, Enrolling International Students and Exchange Visitors—Issuing Forms I-20 and IAP-66.) Many agencies that sponsor or place international students insist that their students study on a J-1 visa because the J-1 classification includes provisions that encourage students to return home following the conclusion of their studies. For more information on the administration of visa programs, first obtain the Code of Federal Regulations (CFRs) governing visas. The *Adviser's Manual of Federal Regulations Affecting Foreign Students and Scholars* can help you understand the CFRs; it is available through NAFSA.

Training Graduate Students as Teaching Assistants

If your institution uses international graduate students as teaching assistants, the students will need an introduction to U.S. teaching and learning mores, grading practices, plagiarism policies, and the consequences of cheating in the classroom. As not all students from abroad have had experience with the software programs commonly used in the United States, practice in computing skills may also be required. Many U.S. universities offer such programs in the month prior to the start of classes in the fall.

Good language skills are particularly pertinent for graduate students with teaching responsibilities. Although personal interviews may be useful for satisfying faculty members' needs for communication, they may not be sufficient to measure students' ability to teach or write a dissertation. It is best to obtain professional assessments of language competency. Further information can be gathered by visiting the TOEFL web site at http://www.toefl.org.

Creating a Successful International Graduate Student Recruitment Plan

The first step in any recruitment plan is to conduct an internal audit. If good baseline statistics about graduate enrollment are not available, it will be difficult to assess whether resources spent on recruitment have had any effect. The audit should include the departmental capacity, current enrollments, recruitment budget, academic and housing facilities, on-campus services, identification of faculty who have international ties or connections, the status of the international alumni records, and an assessment of current international graduate students and their success at the institution. (See chapter 2.2, Creating a Strategic Plan.)

Start by recruiting among current international undergraduates. A certain percentage of your graduate enrollment will be students who continue on for a second degree at your institution; with a minimum of effort, you can seek out the best students, rather than lose them to another institution. If you are not sure how your graduate students learned about your institution, find out by conducting a short, easy-to-answer survey. Include questions that reveal how students heard about your academic programs, how they were recruited, what convinced them to attend your institution, and suggestions they have for recruiting in their country of origin.

Analyze the pools of graduate inquiries and applications to track student interest by source and discipline. Compare data for related departments (for example, sociology and anthropology) to see if inquiries or sources can be shared. Such data are often kept at the departmental level, making analysis difficult; however, gathering these statistics will help in determining where your university is well known and where further promotional work may be needed. It also creates a database to use in follow-up mailings.

Study the international market. Get to know more about the countries from which graduate students come, field by field. Note the states and types of institutions in which international students enroll. The best source of such information is IIE's *Open Doors*, published annually. Understanding where students come from and where they go will help in the assessment of whether active recruitment is realistic for your institution and the type of activities that will be successful.

Design and implement a proactive, well-balanced international graduate student recruitment program. This program may focus on particular countries abroad or on attracting students to particular majors at your university. In either case, select target countries and target universities abroad in which to recruit. Recognize that it may take several years to build a successful program and show results. Ideally, the recruitment plan will include the following:

- An analysis of the history of student flows from target countries

- Past success your institution has had with those countries

- The lists of target universities in countries from which the university would like to attract students

- The cost of travel to those countries over the next three to five years

- An analysis of the potential outcomes of success (in enrollment figures and actual dollars)

- A timeline for the recruiting program

- Possible funding sources to support the recruitment program

- An analysis of potential outcomes should your institution choose not to recruit international students (Use U.S. demographic information for your analysis.)

The Graduate Record Examination (GRE) program provides a service called GRE Search Service for buying prospective student names by discipline. Requests for names can be sorted by the self-reported information given at the time of test registration and the test results, much like the SAT Student Search Service for undergraduates. On average, 22 percent of the students taking the GRE are from countries other than the United States. They are included in the Search Service unless they specifically request that their names be excluded. Students who do not take the test may register for the search service on the GRE web site at http://www.gre.org. During the 1998-99 search cycle, GRE anticipated having 250,000 students in the search service. The GRE Search Service bulletin lists helpful statistics about past student volumes, intended majors, preferred study location, and degree objective to help make decisions on search criteria or whether the search service will be useful to your institution. Information on cost for participation in the GRE Search Service is available on GRE's web site.

Decide what is best for your institution when considering whether to employ "armchair" or active recruitment activities. (See section 3, Recruitment Techniques.) At the graduate level, if international students are seen as a significant part of the student body, it is important to learn more about the institutions from which the students come so that traveling to their countries will have great benefits for the faculty. It is also possible to use the trip as an opportunity to evaluate the possibilities for collaboration on research projects, attract postdoctoral students who can assist with research projects, and recruit prospective faculty.

Establish contact with key faculty in strong departments in target universities. Keep them informed of the growth and development of the university's academic programs. Be sure to contact them well in advance of any travel so that they may prepare students for interviews.

Establish a Graduate Recruitment Committee

Involve faculty at every stage of planning and enlist their active support in implementing strategies. Develop an advisory board or committee of faculty in the disciplines to be targeted. Suggestions from the staff most likely to be affected by the outcome of the recruitment effort is very beneficial. The committee should include some personnel from related disciplines, some of whom have experience in recruiting internationally. It should also include faculty of foreign extraction who can advise the committee of appropriate means of contact in the target countries.

Members of the committee can share their experience, expertise and, most important, their international contacts (e.g., former Fulbright scholars, research associates). For example, they should be involved in determining how data will be collected, deciding on the best methods for recruitment, and identifying who will recruit.

Members of the committee can consider how to share the information gathered during recruitment activities. It may be that one school has too many inquiries and another not enough so sharing inquiries may be appropriate as students abroad may be open to hearing of degree programs they had not previously considered, particularly at the master's degree level. Sharing names of qualified applicants in related fields when a particular program cannot accommodate all those who apply may also be successful.

Application Materials and Publicity

Consider developing a common application for all graduate disciplines at the university. It is the application pool that makes the department unique, not the application. A committee of graduate faculty may be able to agree on pertinent common questions so that all departments can use one form, which can be easily distributed and placed on the web.

Be sure the university web site has complete information about academic programs and research projects for international students. Link departmental web pages to the international student services office web site so students can obtain answers about visas, arrival information, orientation, hosts, housing, other students from their country, and so on.

Consider advertising in professional journals. This method is effective because it targets the people who are most likely to be interested in further study. Journal readers are serious professionals and opinion makers.

International Travel and Education Fairs

There are many public educational fairs held abroad to promote U.S. higher education (see chapter 3.4, Education Fairs). People seeking degree information at both the graduate and undergraduate levels attend these. If traveling overseas, consider going at the time Fulbright fairs are offered on various continents, usually in October and November of each year. Investigate whether the fair is focusing on undergraduate or graduate degree programs. Where there are no Fulbright fairs, consider those sponsored by IIE, the U.S. Foreign Commercial Service and private firms such as NEXUS, Study in the USA, International Conferences, Exhibitions, and Fairs (ICEF), and others. The fairs are organized so that there is sufficient travel time between events to accommodate appointments (see also chapter 5.4, MBA Programs).

At university fairs, those representing graduate departments must have a thorough knowledge of highly sophisticated curricula, research areas, admission criteria, and possible financial support for all departments. Representatives should carry a directory showing faculty specialties, addresses, telephone and fax numbers, and e-mail addresses. Where feasible, the presence of a faculty member from the most targeted field(s) can increase the event's effectiveness. Because many fairs have general sessions on topics of broad interest to attendees, the faculty member might volunteer to do a presentation, thereby giving the institution a public relations advantage.

When traveling, make appointments with department chairs at local universities, established placement agencies, and government officials who might potentially sponsor students (Ministers of Science and Technology, Human Resources, Finance, Transportation, Education, and so on). These contacts will take on greater significance as potential graduate students turn to faculty and counseling centers for advice about pursuing further study in the United States. It is also useful to visit with the staff at the local Fulbright commission.

Survey faculty to find out who is planning to travel abroad to attend conferences, conduct research, or even to take vacation. They may be able to make contacts on behalf of the university in countries not specifically targeted for minimal additional cost. (See chapter 4.1, Building an On-Campus Recruitment Team, and the On-Campus Recruitment Team Questionnaire in appendix F.)

If conducting general recruitment on behalf of many programs, identify personnel who can represent a broad spectrum of graduate programs. They will have to be prepared to answer questions about a number of disciplines, not just their own. If targeting specific academic disciplines, narrow the recruitment activities to locating students specifically for those majors. The latter approach is more labor intensive, but meeting prospective students in their environment, having personal interviews, and meeting their supervising faculty will pay long-term benefits. Target students who are in their last two years of study in order to develop a pipeline of interested students.

An economical method of identifying international graduate students is to form an alliance with the undergraduate recruitment staff who are traveling overseas to meet prospective students. Many parallel functions and techniques have allowed some undergraduate admission staff to be successful representatives for both undergraduate and graduate programs. Generally, if that person is an experienced, well-trained, seasoned professional who is knowledgeable about academic programs at all levels of all departments, it can work. This requires training because the person must have special knowledge of the research projects, decision-making process, and fellowship possibilities in the targeted departments. Although not all undergraduate admission offices see this as part of their mission, it is an institutional investment that maximizes the resources spent on recruitment. Many leads obtained by the undergraduate recruitment staff have turned into successful graduate student enrollments.

Make overseas alumni (U.S. alumni living abroad as well as international alumni) an integral part of the program. Be sure international alumni records are kept up to date. Keep former students informed of the developments in university academic programs. Former students are your best recruiters.

The recruitment of international graduate students should be a planned and well-managed activity. It is a question of whether the institution is managing the population or the population is managing the institution. Lack of management results in skewed populations and lack of assurance that the best students are being recruited. As with the undergraduate population, knowledge of the market is important and personal attention to students will result in the most successful program.

Notes

1. According to the 1997 *National Center for Education Statistics Digest of Education Statistics*, in 1995 there were 2,030,000 students enrolled in graduate and first professional degree programs in the U.S. In 1996–97, there were 196,795 international students enrolled in graduate and first professional degree programs.

2. Data in this section was taken from *Open Doors* 1998/99. New York, N.Y.: Institute of International Education. 1999.

Recruiting for master of business administration (MBA) programs is different from other recruitment efforts. On the surface it might appear easier; anyone who has stood at an international university fair for at least an hour will confirm that a high percentage of the attendees seem to want MBAs. Despite the apparent enthusiasm of fair attendees, recruiting appropriate candidates for MBA programs is more challenging than one might expect.

The MBA on the Educational Landscape

From an educational point of view, the MBA is an anomaly. Every country has its own educational system and tradition. Even national systems that have evolved from British or French models have developed indigenous characteristics that make them unique. Yet the MBA seems to be an international commodity whose shape depends less on the educational tradition of the host country and more on the influence of other MBA programs. As a result, MBA programs worldwide share similar curricula, reading lists, and pedagogies (such as the case method and team projects).

Remarkably, the MBA curriculum is often taught in English, even at universities where all other programs are taught in another language. Some universities will offer two MBA programs—one in the native language and another in English.

The other intriguing characteristic of MBA programs is that they often exist apart from a university. In the United States, schools like The American Graduate School of International Management (Thunderbird) and The Arthur D. Little School of Management offer only graduate study in management: there are no undergraduate programs, no other graduate programs beyond the study of management and administration, and no doctoral programs. Many of the new MBA schools that have opened abroad have followed this model. Prestigious schools such as INSEAD, the international business school, in France; International Institute for Management Development (IMD) in Switzerland; Instituto de Estudios Superiores en Administracion (IESA) in

Venezuela; and Instituto Centroamericana de Administracion de Empresas (INCAE) in Costa Rica, are freestanding graduate business schools.

Challenges to Recruiting for MBA Programs

The MBA was introduced in the United States. It was not considered a particularly prestigious or necessary degree until recent years, when it suddenly became a hot commodity worldwide. Until recently, MBA programs were concentrated in the United States; thus, they became a powerful draw for international students anxious to take their place in an increasingly global economy. By obtaining an MBA degree in the United States, young people demonstrated implicitly their capacity to succeed in another culture and their mastery of English. Their return on investment was quite high, evidenced by the positions open to them in the international corporations that seemed to be opening offices everywhere. Many of those corporations were based in the United States and recruited heavily from U.S. business schools.

Not surprisingly, it didn't take long for new MBA programs to appear. The proliferation of MBA programs worldwide now makes it quite challenging for U.S. schools to claim distinguishing characteristics that would provide an obvious competitive edge. In other words, a Thai student who wishes to earn an MBA, learn how to work and live in another culture in the process, and master English can enroll in a comparable program in Rotterdam, Barcelona, London, Melbourne, Fontainebleau, or Chicago. The MBA may be the first degree that truly reflects a global educational community.

One enormous challenge for MBA programs is the extent to which international students rely on rankings. If you work at a top-ranked school, recruiting overseas is easier. While few educators are comfortable with the efficacy of rankings as a means to distinguish one academic program from another, rankings have a powerful influence on prospective students. International MBA candidates are looking for schools with cachet. They know that they are not the only ones studying the rankings. It is a brave student who will choose to attend a program abroad that is unknown to others in his or her home country.

The university's reputation is often more influential than the ranking of the MBA program. When the university is well known in a country, then its MBA program will be more attractive. If a university has many alumni (regardless of their degree program) in a particular country, that country is likely to be a strong market for the MBA program. The other implication of the linked prestige of the university is that prospective students expect all representatives of a university to have broad and deep knowledge about that university as a whole. Representatives who expect to have any credibility in the international

MBA market are well advised to learn as much as possible about their university (for example, support services for international students, other graduate programs that might enroll the MBA candidate's wife or husband, numbers of undergraduates from different countries, and so on). It is important to link the MBA program to the larger university.

If your school is not at the top of the rankings, you must distinguish it from others, emphasizing the unique opportunities of your programs. Characteristics that attract attention might be the length of the program, dual-degree opportunities or unique specializations (such as business and law, hospital administration, or hotel administration), international focus, corporate consulting projects, geographic location, or cost. These competitive advantages should be highlighted in your literature, in your communication with prospective candidates, and in communications with those who help promote your programs.

There are four logical sources of local support, one of which—alumni—has even more local credibility than the rankings. The other sources are overseas educational advising centers (see chapter 4.3, Resource Networks Overseas: Educational Advisers and Guidance Counselors), test-preparation centers, and local universities. More will be said about each of these below.

Finding the Market

Although university MBA fairs are very popular, it isn't always easy to find candidates appropriate for your program.

MBA admission officers often overlook their most obvious and promising markets—international graduates of undergraduate programs at their university and the friends of alumni. MBA programs enroll individuals from a broad range of professional fields. The management skills taught in MBA programs are important to engineers, accountants, journalists, lawyers, and specialists in international affairs, as well as to graduates of the undergraduate program in business. Several years after earning an undergraduate degree, many alumni find themselves moving into more senior positions within their organizations and are often ready for graduate study. These are people who are already familiar with the campus and its environs, have established relationships with people at the university that they continue to value, and are the most inclined to appreciate the value of a degree earned abroad.

Alumni and their friends are a very logical place to begin any recruitment strategy. Recent alumni are likely to have friends and colleagues who are considering graduate study abroad. The challenge is finding ways to communicate with this group and to integrate them into your recruitment strategy. Coordinate activities with the alumni office and undergraduate admission office so multiple departments do not badger alumni. (See chapter 4.2, Making the Most of Alumni Contacts.)

For traveling admission officers who recruit undergraduate students overseas, a visit to the international and American high schools is the logical way to target the bulk of the U.S.-bound market. For most graduate programs, students enter immediately upon completing their undergraduate program, so a visit to the appropriate department at a foreign university would reach that market. But most MBA schools want to enroll individuals with at least two years of work experience. That means that the best candidates are scattered among hundreds of employers in any given city at any given time. Although some employers encourage young managers to pursue an MBA and, in some cases, even sponsor them, others would not welcome the news that an employee was planning to leave. As a result, employers are not always useful contacts on a recruitment trip.

Prospective MBA students inevitably find their way to the overseas advising center where they will register for the Graduate Management Admissions Test (GMAT) and the TOEFL. It is wise to make certain that overseas advising centers have information and applications for your programs, and even wiser to establish a relationship with the individual advisers in the center. These professionals are an important link between your program and the local market. Like your alumni, educational advisers have the credibility to help candidates look beyond the rankings and consider programs that offer appropriate opportunities for their individual needs. Nearly all overseas advisers now have e-mail addresses, and many attend NAFSA's annual conference, where they welcome the chance to meet admission representatives and increase their knowledge of individual programs. For university representatives who travel alone internationally, the advising centers are an important stop.

Finally, there has been an explosion of private centers that provide orientation to the admission tests. Some of these centers also offer advising. Admission officers should make every effort to learn as much as possible about how these centers operate, the qualifications of their staff, the promises they make to their clients, their fees, and their record of success. Sometimes the local educational advising center or alumni can help. Although some test-related centers operate with the highest professional and ethical standards, others do not. A good relationship with a good test-prep center is a great way to promote and develop visibility for your school; on the other hand, a relationship with an unethical or incompetent center can do irreparable harm.

Collaboration with a local university often provides multiple advantages. The benefits generally come in the long term. Student exchanges, faculty exchanges, and joint case-writing all help to enhance the local visibility and attractiveness of your school abroad and provide tremendous educational advantages back on your home campus.

Tours and Fairs

Several organizations offer events and activities overseas for MBA recruitment. Signing up for a fair or tour overseas may be the easiest way to jump into the international market. Fairs generally draw from several hundred to several thousand students and provide a forum that will give your program much public exposure. Keep in mind that for a school that has very little history in a country, participation in the fair alone may not be sufficient to produce a dramatic shift in international enrollment; most important is building visibility, credibility, and prestige, which generally requires persistence.

Appendix A

NAFSA: Association of International Educators

PRINCIPLES FOR INTERNATIONAL EDUCATIONAL EXCHANGE

Principles for Institutions

The movement of students and scholars across community, cultural, geographic, and national boundaries has been recognized for centuries as essential to the discovery of truth, new knowledge, and the means of applying what is learned abroad to human enrichment and progress. In the second half of this century the interchange of students and scholars has grown steadily, become more formalized and [exerted] an increasing influence upon U.S. higher education and the society as a whole. Indeed, the significance of the interdependence of nations, peoples, and world systems has brought international education into the very mainstream of higher education planning and requirements.

Programs of international educational exchange take many forms and are located in institutions of divergent purposes, sizes, and settings. Regardless of form and content, the value of any program can be realized only when a college or university has made a conscious decision to be involved in international educational exchange and has made a commitment of resources commensurate with the nature and scope of that exchange. Such recognition and commitment require adherence to the following institution-wide principles:

1. The institution should have a clearly stated policy, endorsed by the governing board, setting forth the goals and objectives of the international educational exchange program or programs developed by the institution. This policy should be manifest in the institution's planning and budgeting. Personnel and program resources—administrative and academic—should be sufficient to assure that the program can be operated in ways consistent with the principles presented in this document.
2. The executive staff of the institution should discuss with the faculty and administrative staff the implications of the international educational exchange policy for the academic programs and academic staff.
3. Programs in international educational exchange should be closely related to and consistent with the basic purposes and strengths of the institution.
4. Regardless of program size, the institution should acknowledge its responsibility to demonstrate sensitivity to cultural needs—social, religious, dietary, and housing. These factors must be accounted for in the planning and execution of the program.
5. Special services required by involvement in international educational exchange should be performed by personnel who are trained for their particular responsibilities, and institutional policy should ensure that faculty and administrative staff receive appropriate training for the activities they manage.
6. Administrative staff and faculty should seek to develop and maintain respect and sensitivity toward those from different cultures in the execution of their responsibilities for international educational exchange programs.
7. The institution should periodically evaluate programs, policies, and services, in light of established goals, and regularly review those goals.

Principles for the Admission of Foreign Students

Foreign citizens have usually been educated in school systems that vary from those in the United States. As a result, students from other countries are often unfamiliar with U.S. procedures and terminology. Institutions that admit foreign students must develop a sensitive and flexible admissions policy that reflects an awareness of different academic backgrounds and personal expectations.

To assist institutions in establishing a sound admissions policy and an effective admissions system, criteria for ethical recruitment were developed at a Wingspread colloquium in March 1980. These criteria, known as the "Wingspread Principles," are presented in Foreign Student Recruitment: Realities and Recommendations, and are incorporated in the following principles:

1. The admissions goals and policies for foreign students should be related directly to overall institutional goals and policies and include:
   - The academic characteristics of students to whom admission is offered.
   - The level—graduate or undergraduate—of students sought.
   - Geographical areas to be emphasized or discouraged.
   - The number of students desired (as a proportion of the student body).
   - The extent to which the institution will make financial resources available to foreign students.
2. Admissions materials should be thorough, complete, and clearly written; they should be sensitive to candidates' unfamiliarity with U.S. education and lack of facility in the English language. Care should be taken to include:
   - Detailed information about the admissions requirements and procedures.
   - Candid, pertinent, and current information so that students unfamiliar with U.S. higher education may make informed academic judgments.
   - Realistic information about full costs of study and living expenses, as well as the availability of financial aid.
   - English-language requirements and, if admitted initially for an English-language training program, the degree of commitment the institution accepts for subsequent education of the student in another of its academic programs.
   - Specific information about requirements of academic programs.
   - Complete information regarding the conditions of admissions and acceptance, deposits, orientation, and all steps to be followed prior to arrival.
3. Recruitment of foreign students for both academic and English-language training programs must be conducted in an ethical, responsible manner.

   The student's educational goals must be ascertained and a responsible judgment made about whether they can be achieved at the accepting institution.

   Admissions decisions should be made using complete files including academic documents, English proficiency reports, and other supporting materials.

   Admissions responsibilities, including issuance of the visa eligibility certificate, should never be delegated to third parties outside the institution.

   Applicants to an English-language training program must be given full information about the extent of the institution's commitment to admit such applicants subsequently to another of its academic programs or provide assistance in obtaining admission to another institution.
4. The foreign admissions process should be conducted by personnel who are trained and competent in the interpretation of foreign educational records. These duties may be conducted on a full- or part-time basis as required by the size of the effort.

   At the undergraduate level, foreign student admissions—usually a highly centralized process—should be enhanced by faculty advice.

   In foreign graduate admissions, where deans' offices and faculty committees often play an important role, the advice and recommendations of admissions staff should be carefully considered in the decision process. The important contribution each individual can bring to the admissions decision should be recognized.

   Special reference resources should be acquired and new materials acquired as they become available.

   Admissions personnel should call on the expertise of individuals on the campus, elsewhere, or abroad who can assist in providing sound evaluations.
5. The functions of the admissions office should be coordinated with those units responsible for English-language training, academic programs, and student advising services, and there should be regular contact and sharing of information among those responsible for these functions.

6. The institution's foreign student program should be studied periodically in order to formulate any needed adjustments to admissions criteria, procedures, and processes:

Entering characteristics should be correlated periodically with student retention and other measures of performance.

Students should be queried periodically about reactions to admissions materials and procedures.

Other campus offices as well as cooperating agencies should be queried about the effectiveness of the admissions materials and procedures.

Principles for English Programs and Determination of English Proficiency

An extremely important factor in determining whether the presence of foreign students at a college or university will be a mutually beneficial experience for the students and the institution is the students' ability to use the English language. A student who cannot communicate adequately with faculty, staff, or fellow students will encounter significant difficulties in carrying out even limited daily activities. Moreover, serious deficiencies in English will hamper a student in pursuing an academic program at any level. For those students serving as graduate teaching assistants, the ability to speak English effectively in a classroom is especially critical.

For these reasons, an institution must carefully evaluate the English proficiency (overall ability to use the language) of prospective students when they are being considered for admission. In evaluating English proficiency, both level and field of study should be considered, since the most critical question to be answered is how well the student will be able to cope with a specific program at a given institution. Students whose English proficiency seems adequate for a regular academic program often need an English support course or courses in order to function more efficiently in the classroom or to meet an institutional English requirement. Institutions that maintain a policy of admitting foreign students who are qualified academically but who have limited or minimal skills in English must provide half-time or full-time (intensive) programs in English as a second language or refer students to English training programs where they can receive adequate instruction.

In an effort to establish guidelines by which institutions can evaluate their own or other English programs, NAFSA supports the following principles. These standards apply first to the question of determining English language proficiency and then to the training programs themselves. Except where specifically noted, these principles are meant to apply both to academic institutions and to private, proprietary organizations that offer English training programs.

Determining English Proficiency

The procedures and criteria established for determining English proficiency should be clearly defined. While these procedures should be uniform and comprehensive, they must take into consideration differences presented by at least three common situations:

- For students being admitted directly from overseas, English proficiency should be determined on the basis of results from widely accepted tests designed for this purpose.
- For students who have enrolled in intensive English-language programs conducted by the institution to which they are applying, additional information should be sought regarding the students' overall use of English, specific strengths and weaknesses, and motivation for continued improvement. In this regard there should be close communication between the admissions office and the English language program.
- For students who have been enrolled in intensive English-language programs at other institutions or at private language schools, similar information indicating level of English-language proficiency should be sought. Admissions personnel should seek the assistance of any specialists in English as a second language at their institutions for guidance in interpreting such information.

Institutions should periodically assess their capacity to successfully determine English proficiency of prospective foreign students in light of the students' performance in subsequent academic programs.

English Support Courses

Students with sufficient command of English to begin regular academic work at a college or university frequently require additional training to prepare them for tasks encountered during their program of studies. This training is best provided through English support courses taken in conjunction with regular academic courses in the students' fields. These English courses should address the special needs of students whose native language is not English. They typically range from courses which are the equivalent of freshman English to advanced courses in technical English for graduate students.

After admission, the institution should employ effective procedures to identify those students who require some specialized training in English in light of the specific course of studies to be pursued. Special care should be taken to provide training in oral English skills for foreign graduate students assigned as teaching assistants.

Support courses should be designed and taught by individuals with training in the teaching of English as a second language.

Intensive English Programs

The purpose of an intensive English program is to develop and strengthen the English skills of persons whose native language is not English, usually in preparation for pursuing an academic program at the graduate or undergraduate level. Such individuals generally do not have sufficient command of English to begin regular academic work at a college or university. Some programs administered by colleges and universities enroll only students who have received academic admission to the institution but require short-term training, often in the summer. Most programs at academic institutions maintain year-round schedules and enroll people at varying levels of proficiency who intend to enter degree programs at the same or other institutions. Finally, a large number of programs are administered by private organizations. These latter programs, often housed at academic institutions, enroll students who must all continue their academic studies elsewhere. Based on experience from many established programs, it is not unrealistic to expect students who begin at the lowest levels to require a full calendar year to reach levels of proficiency sufficient to begin academic work.

Intensive English programs should establish clear goals and objectives for the training they provide. In the most general terms, these goals would be to provide sufficient and appropriate training to enable students to meet test score requirements established by the institutions they plan to attend.

In order to achieve these goals, intensive English programs should receive adequate support from their sponsoring institutions. Although no single administrative pattern is required, intensive programs should be sufficiently independent to permit the smooth functioning of all activities and units.

The director and core faculty of an intensive English program should have principal commitments to the program. The director should have advanced academic training in the teaching of English as a second language and have teaching and administrative experience, if possible, including overseas experience. Part-time instructors, especially if they are graduate students in a university program, should be taking or have taken graduate work in the teaching of English as a second language.

To ensure that students will be adequately prepared for an academic program, the syllabus of an intensive English program should include training in a variety of skills. The most basic are listening (understanding spoken English) and reading (understanding written English). Also of importance for academic work are speaking (in both formal and informal settings) and writing (primarily expository writing needed in most fields of study).

Principles for Foreign Student and Scholar Services

An institution that enrolls foreign students or invites foreign scholars should recognize that individuals from different cultures and educational systems have special needs for advice and assistance. These needs must be met by services that are organized, directed, and funded by the host institution. The scope and level of such services is to some extent dependent on the number of foreign students and scholars. Regardless of their number, however, the presence of foreign students and scholars requires certain basic levels of support which enable them to function successfully in U.S. colleges or universities. The following principles concern the provision of these essential services:

1. The host institution should state clearly its intentions to provide special services for the foreign students and scholars it brings to its campus. These services should include:
   - Advisory and counseling services.
   - Mandated and technical services in compliance with U.S. government regulations.
   - Coordination and liaison with the community.
2. Regardless of the number of foreign students and scholars, the level of funding, or other circumstances, there must be one unit in the host institution that is responsible for coordinating these services, and there should be clear and widely acknowledged designation of responsibility for these services.

   These duties may require full- or part-time staff, depending upon the size of the clientele. Where possible, it is highly desirable to have a single individual or office designated to provide these advisory services.

   The staff should be knowledgeable about U.S. immigration law and regulations.
3. The institution should provide ample professional services which are fully accessible to foreign students and scholars. The intention of these services is to assure that maximum benefit is derived from the educational experience. The advisory services must seek to remove impediments and to solve problems on behalf of these individuals.

   The advisory staff must work closely with other campus and community resources which can be of assistance before arrival and throughout the individual's stay.

   An orientation program that introduces students to the physical environment, registration procedures, academic policies, housing, counseling and health services, visa requirements and INS regulations, financial matters, and social and intercultural activities should be provided.

   Advisory services should be provided on an ongoing basis with respect to personal counseling, emergency needs, institutional policies preparation for departure, and reentry to home countries upon completion of stay.

   The advisory staff serve both the institution and the students and scholars it enrolls; they should, therefore, perform an intermediary role and be a channel of communication between those individuals and outside agencies or institutions.

   The advisory staff should seek to bring an intercultural dimension to the educational programs of the institution and the general life of the community.

   Advisory services should include academic advising—performed either by faculty members or foreign student advisers.
4. The advisory staff should exercise their duties in an ethical and professional manner. They must:
   - Adhere to the regulations of the U.S. government, especially those of the Immigration and Naturalization Service.
   - Decline awards and unethical requests for service.

Principles for the Provision of Community Services and Programs

The presence of foreign students and scholars on campus and in the community involves cross-cultural relationships and provides opportunities for increased global awareness. Individual contacts and the sharing of a variety of social and professional activities provide the opportunity for mutual appreciation of different cultural patterns and national aspirations.

Although it may serve a wider constituency at the state or national level, the college or university is an integral part of the community in which it exists. Colleges and universities which enroll foreign students and scholars should make, in cooperation with the community, every effort to assist these students in their adjustment to life in an American community. They may also enhance the education of foreign students and scholars by offering a variety of experiences, both on campus and in the community, which will ensure that optimum benefit is derived from the period of study in the United States.

Institutions should be receptive to approaches from the community and should, if necessary, take the initiative in establishing a relationship with the community (a) to explain the needs of foreign students and scholars, (b) to identify the resources represented by foreign students, and (c) to explore and make full use of the willingness and ability of the community to provide services and programs.

Through the office of the foreign student adviser or its equivalent, institutions should provide assistance, advice, and information as requested by the community for the development of programs and services for foreign students and scholars. These efforts should be evaluated periodically.

Community programs and services should adhere to the following principles:

1. Community groups and organizations should seek to provide programs and services that enhance the experience of the foreign students and scholars while increasing the level of international and intercultural awareness in the community.
2. Community programs and services should be developed in cooperation with the university office that provides on-campus service to foreign students and scholars. Each should be competently designed and conducted and, where possible, coordinated with other community efforts.
3. Community programs must embrace a sensitivity to, and appreciation of, the religious, cultural, and national backgrounds of foreign participants and a proper regard for confidential personal information that may be offered by foreign and American participants.
4. Community groups and organizations should provide professional training for volunteers and paid staff to ensure that programs are competently administered and community resources effectively used.
5. Community groups and organizations should periodically evaluate their programs, policies, and services in light of their established goals and the changing needs of foreign students and scholars.

Principles for U.S. Study Abroad

One of the most effective ways to increase U.S understanding of other languages and cultures and to improve our ability to function effectively in this interdependent world is to provide individuals with opportunities to study abroad. By living and studying in another country people learn to live with and appreciate different points of view and gain a more global perspective on life's challenges and opportunities.

The institution that endorses the concept of study abroad should provide some form of basic advisory services. Many opportunities exist for American students interested in studying abroad—sponsored programs of their own institution, programs sponsored cooperatively with other institutions, and hundreds of direct opportunities which may or may not have U.S. institutional sponsorship.

Advisory Services for Study Abroad

These principles apply to the delivery of advisory services as well as to the direct administration of a study-abroad program or cosponsorship of a program with other institutions.

Within the context of its overall international educational objectives, an institution should have a clearly stated policy about its intentions and goals for facilitating study abroad.

Recognizing that programs and advising may be handled by various people on campus, there should be a central point of access to useful information about overseas opportunities. A library of essential study-abroad information materials should be maintained.

Faculty and staff members who are responsible for advising should be identified and listed in campus reference literature. These individuals should be given opportunities to develop their abilities to provide sound, knowledgeable, and objective advice about study-abroad programs. Important components of advising include the following:

- Clarifying objectives for wanting to go abroad.
- Identifying opportunities that are educationally sound and culturally beneficial.
- Determining the quality, value, and appropriateness of a particular study-abroad experience.
- Coordinating evaluation of students' educational background with admissions personnel of foreign institutions.
- Understanding the implications of a particular study-abroad experience on graduation requirements, transfer credit, and financial aid.

Returning students should be asked to provide evaluations to enable study-abroad advisers to determine the usefulness of the program for those students and possible future participants in that program, and to evaluate the usefulness of the advisory services they received before going abroad.

Cosponsoring Study-Abroad Programs Administered by Other Institutions

In order to encourage study abroad or broaden the options readily available to its students, a number of institutions have elected to join consortia or cosponsor study-abroad programs in which another institution handles program administration. A consortium or cosponsorship arrangement for study abroad should provide opportunities that are consistent with the institution's overall academic objectives, requirements, and standards; the program should be administered in accordance with the principles for study-abroad program administration (see below); and the home campus role in the cosponsorship should be evaluated periodically by faculty, staff, and students to determine if the objectives are being met.

Administration of Study Abroad Programs

Institutions administer study-abroad programs in order to establish direct control over the development and provision of a specific kind of overseas learning experience. Many different kinds of institutions operate programs, including U.S. colleges and universities, foreign universities and companies, and proprietary organizations. The types of programs and amounts of structure and support services vary tremendously. Despite the wide range, all should be administered according to the following principles.

1. The purposes and specific educational objectives of the program should be carefully developed and clearly stated in the program bulletin and promotional materials.
2. Accurate, honest, and complete information should be provided to prospective applicants describing the nature and scope of the program including its opportunities and limitations, how and where instruction will be given, the relationship if any to a foreign institution, grading practices, significant differences between a home-campus experience and what can be expected abroad, information about local attitudes and mores, local living conditions, and the extent of responsibility assumed by the program for housing participants.
3. Applicants should be screened to ensure that participants have the maturity, adequate language proficiency, academic background and achievement, and motivation necessary for success in the type of program and place of study.
4. The program should include an orientation, both predeparture and ongoing, which assists participants in making appropriate personal, social, and academic adjustments. Programs maintaining centers abroad should provide counseling and supervisory services at the foreign center, with special attention to the problems peculiar to the location and nature of the program.
5. The program should encourage extensive and effective use of the unique physical, human, and cultural resources of the host environment, and the academic rigor of the program should be comparable to that at the home campus. There should be clearly defined criteria and policies for judging performance and assigning credit in accordance with prevailing standards and practices at the home institution.

6. Administrative arrangements (such as housing, transportation, and finances) and support services (such as counseling and health services) made both in the United States and at the program location abroad should be managed effectively by carefully selected and qualified staff who have both appropriate academic and administrative experience necessary to perform the work.

7. Programs should be evaluated periodically by student participants, program administrators, and a faculty advisory committee to determine the extent to which objectives and purposes are being met. Changes should be made in light of the findings.

CODE OF ETHICS

Institutional and individual members of NAFSA: Association of International Educators are dedicated to providing high quality education and services to participants in international educational exchange. They represent a wide variety of institutions, disciplines, and services. A code of ethics which proposes to set standards for the professional preparation and conduct of all NAFSA members must accommodate this diversity. This document sets forth a number of general guidelines for ethical conduct applicable to all NAFSA members and then details principles pertaining to many of the various activities members undertake.

Whether paid or unpaid for their work in international educational exchange, all NAFSA members are expected to uphold professional standards.

International educators operate in complex environments, with many legitimate and sometimes competing interests to satisfy. Ultimately, their allegiance must be to the long-term health of international educational exchange programs and participants.

Sorting through ethical dilemmas is often best done with help from others, either one's superiors in the organization or experts in the one's subject-matter area.

1. NAFSA Members Have a Responsibility to:

a. Maintain high standards of professional conduct.

b. Balance the wants, needs, and requirements of program participants, institutional policies, laws and sponsors, having as their ultimate concern the long-term well-being of international educational exchange programs and participants.

c. Resist pressures (personal, social, organizational, financial, and political) to use their influence inappropriately. Refuse to allow considerations of self-aggrandizement or personal gain to influence their professional judgments.

d. Seek appropriate guidance and direction when faced with ethical dilemmas. Make every effort to ensure that their services are offered only to individuals and organizations with a legitimate claim on those services.

2. In Their Professional Preparation and Development, Members Shall:

a. Accurately represent their areas of competence, education, training and experience.

b. Recognize the limits of their expertise and confine themselves to the performance of duties for which they are properly trained and qualified, making referrals when situations are outside their area of competence.

Since they work in an area affected by rapid social, political and economic changes, members must make constant efforts to keep current in order to be professionally competent.

c. Be informed of current developments in their fields, and ensure their continuing development and competence.

d. Stay abreast of developments in laws and regulations that affect their clients.

e. Actively uphold the Association's code of ethics when practices that contravene it become evident.

3. In Relationships with Students and Scholars, Members Shall:

a. Understand and protect the civil and human rights of all individuals. Not discriminate with regard to race, national origin, color, gender, religion, sexual orientation, age, political opinion, immigration status, or disability.

b. Recognize their own cultural and value orientations and be aware of how those orientation affect their interactions with people from other cultures.

c. Demonstrate awareness of, sensitivity to and respect for other educational systems, values and cultures.

d. Not exploit, threaten, coerce, or sexually harass students or scholars.

e. Refrain from invoking immigration regulations in order to intimidate students or scholars in matters not related to their immigration status.

f. Maintain the confidentiality, integrity, and security of student records and of all communications with students. Secure permission of the student or scholar before sharing information with others inside or outside the organization, unless disclosure is authorized by law or institutional policy, or mandated by previous arrangement.

g. Refrain from becoming involved in personal relationships with particular students and scholars when such relationships might result in either the appearance or the fact of undue influence being exercised on the making of professional judgments.

h. Respond to inquiries fairly, equitably, and professionally.

i. Seek qualified assistance for students or scholars who appear to be experiencing unusual levels of emotional difficulty.

j. Accept only those gifts which are of nominal value and which do not seem intended to influence the manner in which professional responsibilities are exercised, while remaining sensitive to the varying significance and implications of gifts in different cultures.

k. Assure the provision of information and support services needed to facilitate participants' adaptation to a new educational and cultural environment.

4. In Professional Relationships, Members Shall:

a. Show respect for the diversity of viewpoints found among colleagues, just as they show respect for the diversity of viewpoints among their clients.

One of the most challenging aspects of work in the field of educational exchange is balancing among the dictates of various cultures and value systems. Members need to be well aware of the influence that culture has had on their own values and habits, and on the interpretations and judgments they make of the thoughts and habits of others.

While enjoying interpersonal dealings with people from other cultures, members need to avoid situations in which their judgments may be or appear to be clouded as a result of personal relationships—either positive or negative ones—with particular exchange participants.

Although a categorical ban on accepting gifts would be inappropriate for members who work with individuals representing cultures where the giving of gifts is important, members need to exercise caution in accepting gifts that might be intended to influence them as they carry out their duties.

Being tolerant and respectful of differences in behavior and values among culturally similar others is often more difficult than being tolerant of those differences when they are manifested by people from other cultures. Nevertheless, members should make every effort to show their same-culture colleagues the respect they show their different-culture clients.

Just as they have duties to their clients, members have duties to their professional colleagues. When members accept responsibilities through the Association, they should carry them out with dispatch.

b. Refrain from unjustified or unseemly criticism of fellow members, other programs, and other organizations.

c. Use their office, title, and professional associations only for the conduct of official business.

d. Make certain when participating in joint activities that collaborators receive due credit for their contributions.

e. Carry out, in a timely and professional manner, any Association responsibilities they agree to accept.

5. When Administering Programs, Members Shall:

a. Clearly and accurately represent the goals, capabilities, and costs of the programs.

In the press of daily business, it is often tempting to overlook the long-term need for professional development. Members need to remain cognizant of the need for continuing professional development.

b. Recruit individuals who are qualified to offer the instruction or services promised, train and supervise them responsibly, and assure by means of regular evaluation that they are performing acceptably and that the overall program is meeting its professed goals.

c. Strive to establish standards, activities, and fee structures which are appropriate and responsive to participant needs.

d. Encourage and support participation in professional development activities.

6. In Making Public Statements, Members Shall:

a. Clearly distinguish, in both written and oral public statements, between personal opinions and opinions representing the Association, their own institutions, or other organizations.

b. Provide accurate, complete, current, and unbiased information.

7. Members with Admissions Responsibilities Shall:

a. Consider the welfare of both potential and actual applicants as their primary responsibility.

Many colleges and universities concerned with ethical recruitment limit their representation abroad to staff and/or carefully selected and briefed alumni.

NAFSA members entering into formal or informal contractual relationships for purposes of international student recruitment would be well advised to:
1) be prudent in evaluating agents prior to contracting by soliciting information from students, other clients of the agent and other sources available;
2) obtain written confirmation that the agent is aware of the NAFSA code of ethics and subscribes to the standards it contains;
3) monitor the performance of their agents in light of these standards;
4) terminate agent relationships when it becomes evident that there is a pattern of substandard practice.

b. Adhere to the following guidelines for the ethical recruitment of foreign students:
(1) Provide enough candid and pertinent information that a foreign student unfamiliar with United States practices in higher education may make informed academic judgments.
(2) Develop an admissions policy for foreign students which requires that admissions judgments be made by institutional personnel who rule on other admissions, is based on a system of written criteria, and is applied in competition with other applicants.
(3) Seek a match between the needs and aspirations of the prospective student and

the educational opportunities the institution affords.

(4) Accept the commitment to provide effective educational opportunity for foreign students and establish appropriate institutional policies governing foreign student recruitment, admissions, support activities, specialized programs and curricula.

(5) Provide realistic estimates of costs for tuition, educational expenses, subsistence and related fees and of the extent to which financial aid or scholarships are available to foreign students.

(6) Restrict evaluation of foreign academic records to personnel who are trained and competent in interpretation of foreign educational records.

(7) State clearly to students admitted to English language programs the extent of commitment made for their further education in the United States.

(8) Contract only with individuals or organizations whose practice conforms to the NAFSA Code of Ethics.

c. Make certain they are well versed in the art of evaluating educational credentials from abroad, employing a thorough knowledge of foreign educational systems.

Irrelevant criteria, such as an applicant's immigration status, should not be applied in making admission decisions.

d. Provide complete, accurate, and current information about their institutions' admissions criteria, educational costs, financial support opportunities, academic programs, and student services, in order to give students who are unfamiliar with local educational practices the basis for an informed choice. Encourage prospective students to make realistic assessments of their prospects for achieving their educational objectives at the member's particular institution.

Members with admission responsibilities sometimes come under pressure to admit applicants whose qualifications do not appear to prepare them for success. Those pressures ought to be resisted.

e. Employ only criteria relevant to a candidate's academic potential, level of language proficiency, educationally relevant special abilities and characteristics, and availability of financial support, in determining admissibility.

f. Resist pressure from institutional officers to admit unqualified applicants.

8. Members with Responsibility for Teaching English as a Second Language Shall:

Members making English-language placement recommendations might ought to base them on evidence of the applicant's linguistic proficiency, not on assumptions based on the applicant's national origin or other irrelevant factors.

a. Employ fair and accurate English proficiency tests in admissions and placement, and then use the test results in the student's best interest, evaluating students based on their individual merits and accomplishments.

b. Use up-to-date methods and materials appropriate to the needs of the specific populations and individuals being instructed.

c. Assure that the instruction they offer concerns not just the linguistic aspects of English, but also cultural aspects, the understanding of which will aid students in achieving their academic goals.

9. Members Who Advise Foreign Students and Scholars Shall:

Members should keep in mind that policies on the confidentiality of information apply to law-enforcement organizations as much as they do to any other type of organization.

a. Clarify the adviser's role to all parties and limit advice to matters within that mandate, making appropriate referrals when necessary.

b. Fully inform students, at appropriate times, of the types of information the institution is required to furnish to governmental agencies, and furnish those agencies with only that information required by law and regulation.

c. Decline to reveal confidential information about foreign students and scholars even if requests for such information come from law enforcement agencies or organizations appearing to have thoroughly benevolent motives.

Members ought not seek to influence their advisees' decisions by withholding information that might help the advisees thoroughly consider alternatives open to them.

d. Assist students and scholars in making prudent decisions, not withholding information that might widen their range of choices and not encouraging illegal actions.

10. Members with Responsibilities in Community Organizations Working with Foreign Students and Scholars Shall:

People who are visiting another country may have no reliable way of knowing about the goals of organizations seeking their participation or affiliation. To assist these visitors, organizations have a responsibility to make their objectives clear.

a. Make certain that organizations providing programs for foreign students and scholars have clear statements of purpose and responsibility, so that all parties can know what is expected of them.

b. Accurately portray their services and programs, making clear the identity, the intent, and the nature of the sponsoring organization and of each particular event or service.

In their efforts to attract an adequate number of domestic participants in such activities as spouse and host family programs, members ought to resist pressures to accept as participants individuals whose motives are less than benevolent.

c. Provide appropriate opportunities to observe and to join in mutual inquiry into cultural differences.

d. Provide adequate orientation for volunteers and participants in community programs so they may understand each other and may interact constructively. The organization should make clear that surreptitious, deceptive or coercive proselytizing is unacceptable.

Members in the study-abroad area sometimes face pressures to meet enrollment goals by accepting or encouraging the participation of students whose potential for benefiting from the program seems limited. These pressures should be resisted.

With the plethora of study abroad programs available, members need to remain mindful that their clients rely upon them for judgments about program quality.

11. Members with Responsibilities in Students Abroad Shall:

a. Provide complete and accurate information to students they advise, in order for students to make informed choices. Seek to ensure that students select overseas opportunities that seem suitable in terms of academic content, location, language preparation, emotional maturity, and cultural variation.

b. Ensure that any promotional materials they make available concern well-documented programs with reputable sponsors.

c. Assure appropriate educational guidance of students bound abroad through orientation and reentry programs and materials.

Original text approved by the NAFSA Board of Directors on May 28, 1989. Revisions approved by the NAFSA Board of Directors on October 5, 1992.

GUIDELINES FOR THE RECRUITMENT, ADMISSION, AND SUPPORT OF INTERNATIONAL STUDENTS

Approved by the Executive Board, November, 1998

The following set of guidelines is based on NACAC's belief that all students, whether United States (U.S.) citizens, U.S. permanent residents, or international students, should be treated fairly in the college admission process. Recognizing that international students and U.S. citizens living outside the United States often face particular issues and concerns when seeking admission to U.S. colleges and universities, these guidelines recommend standards of professional and ethical practice for the recruitment, admission, and support of these students.

It should be noted that, in this document, international students are defined as those holding foreign citizenship who do not have permanent residency status in the U.S. and who will enter the country in a non-immigrant status.

Colleges and Universities Should:

- Carefully delineate and explain the admission process for international students in their literature when those procedures differ from those for domestic students.
- Train staff to be as accurate as possible in responding to student inquiries, remembering that many international students attend school in the U.S. and that many domestic students attend school in other countries. If a particular office or admission officer handles international applicants, identify that office or person in correspondence or literature sent to international students.
- Ensure that students receive accurate information in a timely manner.
- Explain the total cost of attendance, financial aid procedures, deadlines, forms and monetary limitations in clear and precise terms which will allow a prospective student to determine whether the institution can meet his or her financial need. Qualifications and procedures for applying for scholarships should be clearly explained.
- Familiarize coaches, alumni, and all others who recruit for the institution with its admission procedures and with the *Statement of Principles of Good Practice* (SPGP), Section I. A. 3.
- Explain as clearly as possible the level of competitiveness for admission to their institution for international students.
- Consider the use of a preliminary application, if appropriate, to eliminate academically or financially unrealistic candidates from the pool before they invest time and money in applying.
- Not encourage large numbers of students to apply for a very limited number of places.
- Notify candidates as soon as possible if they are clearly inadmissible.
- Be careful in the selection of terminology to describe the admission process, realizing that many words are used only in the U.S. and may not be understood by students in other countries.
- List in the appropriate literature those educational credentials which may permit a students to obtain advanced standing or credit (e.g., International Baccalaureate, British A Levels, German Abitur).
- State which standardized test(s) (e.g., SAT I, SAT II, ELPT, ACT, TOEFL, TWE, TSE) are required for which populations of students (i.e. differentiating between native English speakers and students for whom English is not a first or best language; students for whom English is or is not the language of instruction), by when they must be taken, whether scores must be sent from the testing agency or if scores reported by the school are acceptable, any minimums or cut-off scores used in the admission process, and the relative weight of scores vis-a-vis other indices of academic achievement.

- Refrain from using minimum test scores as the sole criterion for admission, thereby denying certain students because of small differences in scores.
- Be as flexible as possible with deadlines and requirements, remembering that international students must apply for tests much earlier than domestic applicants and that test centers are limited and often become filled.
- Consider carefully institutional policies dealing with English proficiency to ensure that requirements are clear and reasonable.
- Be sensitive to the academic schedules and the needs of students and schools when visiting a secondary school to recruit. Consider traveling with a group of admission officers to minimize the disruption of individual school visits.
- Provide training and resources to admission staff to familiarize them with different academic systems in order to effectively evaluate the applications of international students.
- Recognize that teacher reference forms and school recommendations may be completed from a different perspective than those in the U.S. Institutions must be careful not to penalize students for circumstances which are beyond their control.
- Ensure that all alumni representatives are trained in current admission policies. Encourage them to be sensitive to the schedules and commitments of the students and schools with whom they work.
- Use great caution if the institution chooses to deal with agents and recruiters. Payment or compensation based in any way on a per student recruited basis is explicitly forbidden in the SPGP Sections I. A. 1. and I. A. 5.
- Be as flexible as possible with regard to all deadlines, including the May 1 Candidates Reply Date. Institutions need to be cognizant of very different school calendars abroad which may delay some documentation. Institutions should not fill housing or places in programs in ways that systematically discriminate against applicants from other countries.
- When a student is denied a visa, try to determine the reason for the denial and supply whatever information the Consul requests.
- Develop and implement a support network and system for international students on your campus. There should be advisors who are specially trained to deal with immigration issues, as well as adjustment to U.S. society and to the U.S. educational experience.
- Notify the school counselor or principal of all admission decisions on applicants from that school.

Section II of this document provides guidelines for secondary schools. The complete document is available from the National Association for College Admission Counseling, 1631 Prince Street, Alexandria, VA 22314-2818; tel: 703-836-2222; fax: 703-836-8015.

HOW TO CONTACT AMERICAN AND INTERNATIONAL SCHOOLS OVERSEAS

There are various organizations that support overseas American-style and international schools. These schools are often good starting points for professionals interested in recruiting international students and Americans studying overseas.

FEDERAL AGENCIES

Office of Overseas Schools (AOS)
U.S. Department of State
Room 245, SA-29
Washington, DC 20522-2902
tel: 703- 875 7800
fax: 703-875 7979
e-mail: overseas.schools@dos.us-state.gov
www.state.gov/www/about_state/schools

Department of Defense Education Activity (DoDEA)
4040 N. Fairfax Drive
Arlington, VA 22203-1635
ATTN: Robert Curtis
tel: 703-696 4374 ext. 1923
fax: 703-696 8924
e-mail: robert_curtis@odeadodea.edu
www.odedodea.edu

ASSOCIATIONS

Association for Advancement of
International Education (AAIE)
Thompson House, Westminster College
New Wilmington, PA 16172
tel: 412-946 7192
fax: 412-946 7194
www.aaie.org

International Schools Service, Inc. (ISS)
15 Roszel Road, P.O. Box 5910
Princeton, NJ 08543
tel: 609-452 0990
fax: 609-452 2690
e-mail: iss@iss.edu
www.iss.edu

REGIONAL SCHOOL ASSOCIATIONS

Association of American Schools of
Central America
Columbia, Caribbean, and Mexico
c/o Northwest 73rd Avenue, Suite 021-80138
Miami, FL 33166-6400
(Association is based in Quito, Ecuador)
tel: 593-2-477 534, ext. 114
fax: 593-2-434 985 or 593-2-472 972
e-mail: marysanc@uio.satnet.net
www.tri-association.org

Association of American Schools in
South America (AASSA)
AASSA Regional Development Center
14750 NW 77th Court, Suite 210
Miami Lakes, FL 33016
tel: 305-821 0345
fax: 305-821 4244
e-mail: aassa@gate.net
www.aassa.com

East Asia Regional Council of Overseas
Schools (EARCOS)
P.O. Box 82
Olongapo City Post Office
2200 Philippines
tel: 63-47-252 1321
fax: 63-47-252 1323
e-mail: EARCOS@iskl.po.my
www.earcos.org

European Council of International
Schools (ECIS)
21 Lavant Street
Petersfield, Hampshire
GU32 3EL United Kingdom
tel: 44-1730 268 244
fax: 44-1730 267 914
e-mail: ecis@ecis.org
www.ecis.org

Association of International Schools in
Africa (AISA)
c/o International School of Kenya
P.O. Box 14103
Nairobi, Kenya
tel: 254-2-58 24 21
fax: 254-2-58 24 51
e-mail: Miffie_Greer@isk.ac.ke

Central and Eastern European Schools
Association (CEESA)
c/o The American School of Warsaw
American Embassy Warsaw
Department of State
Washington, DC 20521-5010
tel/fax: 48-22-409 380
e-mail: ceesa@it.com.pl
www.ceesacentral.org

Mediterranean Association of
International Schools (MAIS)
c/o American School of Madrid
Apartado 80
28080 Madrid, Spain
tel: 34-91-357 2154
fax: 34-91-357 2678
e-mail: mais@mais-web.org
www.mais-web.org

Near East South Asia Council for
Overseas Schools (NESA)
c/o The American Colleges of Greece
P.O. Box 60018
153 42 Aghia, Paraskevi
Athens, Greece
tel: 30-1-600 9821
fax: 30-1-600 9928
e-mail: nesa@ath.forthnet.gr
www.nesacenter.org

Source: *The College Board. 1998.* "International Recruitment Kit." New York: College Entrance Examination Board.

Appendix E

RECRUITMENT CALENDAR

This calendar can be used for planning an international individual recruitment trip (see chapter 3.3).

JANUARY

- Involve everyone on your campus.
- Define recruitment objectives.
- Set budget guidelines.
- Review *Open Doors*; compare enrollments and trends with your statistics.
- Request tour information.
- Plan a trip to Washington, DC, to visit sponsoring agencies and embassies.
- Register for a class in a foreign language or in cross-cultural communication.
- Fax applicants whose files are not complete. A fax to their school might also be in order.

FEBRUARY

- Write letters to embassies and sponsoring agencies requesting visits; book hotel and airline reservations.
- Make a list of the countries you want to visit, the names of students from those countries, and the schools they attended.
- Contact faculty and students on campus from those countries and get their opinions about visiting.
- Outline publications needed for recruitment trip; decide what to mail when.
- Process applications and notify applicants as soon as possible.

MARCH

- Contact colleagues and seek information about their recruitment efforts.
- Obtain information about college fairs; choose how, when, and where to participate.
- Decide whether you want to travel individually, in a small group, or with a tour.
- Decide who should travel.
- Outline travel itinerary; check holidays.
- Write copy and collect photographs for new publications.
- Place advertisements in magazines and journals.

APRIL

- Visit Washington, DC
- For individual or small group tours:
  - Make airline and hotel reservations.
  - Plan social functions.
  - Make initial inquiries to schools and educational advising centers.
  - Revise budget.
- Finalize copy for new publications.
- Contact international students and faculty on campus. Give them your schedule. Enlist their assistance while they are home during the summer.
- Contact alumni.

MAY

- Write and request appointments overseas.
- Attend NAFSA Conference and try to meet people from countries you are going to visit. Go to sessions about those countries. Attend pre-conference workshop on recruitment.
- Print new international student materials.
- Register for tours and fairs.
- Ask alumni to assist with fairs.
- Meet with department heads to learn what they are looking for in international students and what they have to offer these students.

JUNE

- Organize the office.
- Prepare tentative schedule based on response.
- Read everything you can about the countries you are going to visit.
- Learn about educational systems.
- Order new school/college directories and build a mailing list.
- Request names from student search programs.

JULY

- Mail publications and videos overseas.
- Obtain passport and visas.
- Continue reading and language class.
- Review budget; develop a plan for paying your bills when you travel.

AUGUST

- Ship additional materials overseas.
- Inform prospective applicants, alumni, and parents of current students of your schedule.
- Send invitations to social functions.
- Mail or fax letters confirming appointments.
- Prepare photo album for the trip.
- Continue reading and buy maps of the cities you are going to visit.

SEPTEMBER

- Finalize itinerary.
- Share your final itinerary with everyone.
- Place newspaper advertisements.
- Plan your packing.
- Obtain traveler's checks.
- Reconfirm airline and hotel reservations.

OCTOBER

Travel
overseas

NOVEMBER

- Send applications, brochures, and catalogues to prospective students.
- Write thank-you letters to all who helped you on the trip.
- Share photographs with current international students and ask them to write to prospective applicants.

DECEMBER

- Write a report of your trip with expense report and inquiry analysis.
- Send the report to everyone.
- Submit budget request for next year.

Source: Linden Educational Services, Washington, D.C.

ON-CAMPUS RECRUITMENT TEAM QUESTIONNAIRE

This sample questionnaire can be used to identify potential team members among faculty and staff for building an on-campus recruitment team (see chapter 4.1).

1. Based on the accompanying description of our recruitment goals and strategies, would you be interested in assisting in our recruitment efforts?

2. Have you worked or are you currently working with international students? In what capacity?

3. Please list any international organizations, associations, and clubs of which you are a current or past member. What is/was your role in the organization?

4. Have you traveled abroad? If so, where did you travel?

5. Please list any international travel plans you have for the coming year. Will you have time during any of your trips to assist with our recruitment efforts?

6. Do you have contacts abroad that might prove helpful with some aspect of the recruiting process? Would they be willing to assist our office?

7. In which of the following activities would you be willing to assist our office?
   - ❒ Network building
   - ❒ College fairs
   - ❒ School visits
   - ❒ Interviews
   - ❒ Receptions
   - ❒ Other _____

THIRD-PARTY RECRUITER/AGENCY QUESTIONNAIRE

Survey previously used by NAFSA to qualify third-party recruiters and agents (see chapter 4.4).

1. Please give the exact official name, address, and telephone number of your agency:

   English   **Native Language**

   _____   _____

   _____   _____

   _____   _____

2. Please list the names and titles of officers of the agency.

   _____   _____

   _____   _____

   _____   _____

3. How many staff members do you have?

   Part-time _____   Full-time _____

4. How many have been educated in the United States? _____

   Please indicate the educational background and experience of the agency's staff.

   U.S. undergraduate degree _____   U.S. graduate degree _____

   U.S. non-degree study _____   Non-U.S. degree _____

5. Does your organization have contractual relationships with other placement or counseling organizations?

   Yes _____ No _____

   If yes, in the United States _____ Overseas _____

6. Do you obtain admission for students at institutions other than those with which you have a contractual agreement?

   Yes _____ No _____

7. If your agency uses other names or has used other names in the past, please list them.

_____   _____

_____   _____

_____   _____

8. What services are provided? (check all that are applicable)
   ____ Placement (seeking admission to U.S. educational programs on behalf of prospective students)
   ____ Recruitment (seeking to attract students to particular institutions or programs)
   ____ Advising/counseling (assisting students in deciding whether an education in the U.S. would be practical for them and would help them attain their educational goals)
   ____ Publications
   ____ Travel arrangements
   ____ Offering ESL
   ____ Arranging homestays
   ____ Job placement
   ____ U.S. educational resource library

9. Do you organize fairs?   Yes _____ No _____

   Do you participate in fairs?   Yes _____ No _____

10. When did your agency begin operation?

_____

11. In which countries (including the U.S.) do you promote your services?

_____   _____

_____   _____

_____   _____

12. To which group(s) do you provide services?
   ____ U.S. institutions
      Two-year ____ Four-year ____ Public ____ Private ____
   ____ Institutions outside the U.S.
   ____ Prospective students
      Your country ____ Other countries ____

13. In what types of academic programs do you seek admission for students?

___	Secondary schools	___	Short-term (ESL, one-term)
___	Two-year institutions	___	Four-year institutions
___	Graduate programs	___	Colleges
___	Universities		

14. How many students were admitted to U.S. schools through your auspices in the last twelve months?

_____

15. From which countries did these students (question 14) come?

_____   _____

_____   _____

_____   _____

16. Please check which types of fees are charged to your clients.
    ___ Fee for counseling/advising
    ___ Fee for admission obtained
    ___ Fee to U.S. institution per student recruited
    ___ Fee to U.S. institution on a per-hour basis
    ___ Fee to U.S. institution on annual retainer basis
    ___ Fee to non-U.S. institution for placement of its students in U.S. programs
    ___ Fees for special programs
    ___ Other

17. Does your agency make specific arrangements with U.S. institutions to admit students to English-language programs?

    Yes _____ No _____

    If so, is the placement for the duration of the English-language training only?

    Yes _____ No _____

18. If students are admitted to English-language programs, do you also make arrangements for the students' subsequent admission to academic programs?

    Yes _____ No _____

19. Does your agency have permission to issue form IAP-66?

    Yes _____ No _____

20. In any contractual agreements with colleges and universities, does your agency have the authority to make admission commitments to students?

Yes _____ No _____

To sign I-20s? _____

21. How does your office verify the accuracy of or provide analysis of a student's academic records?

_____

_____

_____

Questionnaire completed by:

_____
(signature)

_____
(name–print)

_____
(date)

Source: NAFSA: Association of International Educators, Washington, DC